Henry Watkins Allen

The travels of a sugar planter

Six months in Europe

Henry Watkins Allen

The travels of a sugar planter
Six months in Europe

ISBN/EAN: 9783337132217

Printed in Europe, USA, Canada, Australia, Japan

Cover: Foto ©Andreas Hilbeck / pixelio.de

More available books at **www.hansebooks.com**

THE
TRAVELS OF A SUGAR PLANTER.

THE TRAVELS

OF A

SUGAR PLANTER·

OR,

SIX MONTHS IN EUROPE.

BY

H. W. ALLEN.

NEW YORK:
JOHN F. TROW, PRINTER,
48 & 50 GREENE STREET.
1861.

Entered, according to Act of Congress, in the year 1861,
BY J. F. TROW.
In the Clerk's Office of the District Court of the United States for the
Southern District of New York.

TO

"THE GOOD PEOPLE OF THE PARISH OF WEST BATON ROUGE, LA.,

MY FRIENDS,

WHO HAVE EVER GIVEN ME THEIR FULLEST CONFIDENCE
AND HIGHEST ESTEEM,

THIS VOLUME

IS RESPECTFULLY AND GRATEFULLY DEDICATED,

BY THEIR REPRESENTATIVE.

ALLANDALE PLANTATION,
Sept. 25th, 1860.

CONTENTS.

		PAGE
I.	Letter from Liverpool, England,	1
II.	" " Belfast, Ireland,	7
II.	" " Glasgow, Scotland,	14
IV.	" " Bonnie Doon, "	19
V.	" " Edinboro', "	25
VI.	" " London, England,	37
VII.	" " London, "	49
VIII.	" " Paris, France,	64
IX.	" " Geneva, Switzerland,	70
X.	" " Geneva, "	75
XI.	" " Chamouni, "	81
XII.	" " Berne, "	85
XIII.	" " Lucerne, "	91
XIV.	" " Zurich, "	95
XV.	" " Baden-Baden,	103
XVI.	" " Wiesbaden, Germany,	107
XVII.	" " Antwerp, Belgium,	114
XVIII.	" " Amsterdam, Holland,	121
XIX.	" " Berlin,	126
XX.	" " Dresden, Saxony,	137
XXI.	" " Vienna, Austria,	146

CONTENTS.

					PAGE
XXII.	Letter from	Trieste, Austria,	.	.	156
XXIII.	" "	Venice, Italy,	.	.	161
XXIV.	" "	Milan, "	.	.	169
XXV.	" "	Genoa, "	.	.	177
XXVI.	" "	Pisa, "	.	.	184
XXVII.	" "	Florence, "	.	.	190
XXVIII.	" "	Florence, "	.	.	198
XXIX.	" "	Rome, "	.	.	206
XXX.	" "	Rome, "	.	.	214
XXXI.	" "	West Baton Rouge, La.,—Home Again,		.	226
APPENDIX,	.	. . .	.	.	239

TRAVELS OF A SUGAR PLANTER.

LETTER NO. I.

Queen's Hotel, Liverpool, England,
July 16, 1859.

Editors Advocate:

I arrived at this place last evening at sundown, and have availed myself of this earliest opportunity to write you. I find that I shall not be able to write you as often as you requested, but shall from time to time drop you a line, which I trust will at least amuse if not instruct your numerous readers. We left New York on the 6th instant, at 12 o'clock M., on board the royal steamer Persia, and arrived here in nine days and four hours. The trip would have been made in nine days, but we were detained fully four hours in consequence of icebergs off Newfoundland, where we got into quite a nest of these terrors to navigators. While among these dangers of the deep, there was great excitement on board.

There was but little sleeping that night, for we all remembered the melancholy fate of the President, and the very recent terrible accident to the Edinburgh; but the good ship Persia carried us through safe, running at the rate of twenty-four miles an hour! Icebergs are certainly most magnificent-looking objects. They assume every imaginable shape. Some resemble splendid cathedrals, a mile long, while others, like huge square towers, rise many hundred feet above the sea, and seem as solid as if they rested upon the very bottom of the " vasty deep." If they could be divested of their terrors, they certainly would be delightful objects with which to while away the monotony of a sea-voyage.

On shipboard I found many friends and acquaintances from Louisiana. Among them our Senator, Hon. J. P. Benjamin, Gov. P. O. Hebert and lady, C. D. Stewart, Esq., and family, of Point Coupée, Dr. S. A. Smith, of Rapides, Mr. Norton and daughter, of New Orleans, and Hon. George Eustis and lady. We had quite a number of distinguished strangers on board, among whom were Ex-President Comonfort, of Mexico, John Van Buren, and Mr. O'Gorman, the Irish patriot. To all of these I had the honor to be introduced; with two of them I talked politics—the other I entertained, in true West Baton Rouge style, with a small game of *draw poker*.

My friend, the Ex-President, is down upon his native country, and says that the United States will be doing God's service to go at once and take possession of the whole of Mexico. I am decidedly of his opinion; for unless something is done, and that quickly, like the Kilkenny cats, they will eat up one another, and leave the Anglo-Saxon land-robber nothing but the tail end of a once beautiful and rich country. I have spent this day in sight-seeing and giving coppers to beggars; for I must say there are more beggars in Liverpool than in our whole country put together. This being the great commercial emporium of Great Britain, her merchants have paid great attention to shipping, warehouses, docks, wharves, &c., which latter are among the wonders of the world. It well pays one a trip across the Atlantic, simply to see the docks of this great city. They are built of solid masonry, of immense thickness, and will take in vessels drawing twenty-seven feet of water. They extend for eight miles!

Every thing in Liverpool seems to have been built to stand as long as time shall last, with the view of bordering on eternity; for nearly every house is built of fire-bricks and cast-iron! being the very same materials with which we set our sugar kettles, and build our bagasse furnaces. They boast here of the finest concert-hall in all Europe. It is called the St. George, and is a very magnificent affair, far ahead of any thing in our country. The hotels here are all very small, but well kept, having no general eating room, but simply a saloon or coffee-room, where you order your meals as at our restaurants. The roast beef of old England is her pride and her glory, and accounts in a great measure for the bravery of her soldiers on so many well-fought battle-fields. It gives them " a *stomach* for the fight." Then only think of fresh salmon every morning for breakfast, and cherries as large as walnuts! I visited the fish-market this morning, and found many kinds of rare and delicious fish, mostly from the Irish coast. Prince's Park is the favorite promenade for the denizens of this great commercial metropolis. It is a delightful place, and here I first saw that species of green velvet sward, so common in " merrie England," on which the bold bands of Robin Hood were accustomed to sleep. Strange to say, there is no ice here. Although the climate in winter is cold and disagreeable, still, the fogs are so heavy that they seem to prevent that intense cold which is required to make good ice. Even in the coffee-houses or bar-rooms, you can't get any ice. As to a mint-julep, I don't think such a thing was ever seen in Liverpool. The cry is, mug of (h)ale, 'alf and 'alf, 'ot whiskey punch. I find that the English are generally violently opposed to the recent treaty. The press here is unanimous, and without any exception denounces Napoleon and Villa Franca. They abuse him, and even ridicule him; but a passing stranger can easily see that there is an all-pervading secret dread that the Frenchman will some day cross the Channel. I forgot to tell you, that during my voyage I became very sea-sick. After getting well, I composed the following verses, which I send you in order that you may know that you have " a poet among you."

SEA-SICKNESS—A CURE FOR LOVE.

'Tis said that absence conquers love;
  But you, I think, will say with me,
There's nothing that's so sure to prove
  A cure for love, as "going to sea."

"To sigh like furnace," poets say,
  Will heal the heart that's badly bit,
Will drive "all suicides" away,
  Restore again the wandering wit.

Believe it not, but rather think
  The best of ways to ease the heart
Is—go to sea, and take one drink
  Of Neptune's beverage: then you're smart.

I am here now, but how to get back home without crossing the ocean I cannot tell. I wish I could. Oh, those terrible waves! that eternal rocking of the ship, that "d——d compound of villainous smells"—bah! I feel like Mr. John Routh of Texas once did. It was his first trip to Havana. He was very sea-sick the whole voyage, and suffered much. On his arrival he went up to the hotel, and immediately ordered his landlord to send out and buy him a horse. The horse was bought, saddled and bridled; Mr. Routh stood in front of his hotel, looking at his prize with great satisfaction and delight, when a party of friends came up, and wanted, in the name of Heaven, to know what he wanted with a horse. "Why," said he, "I am tired of ships and sea-sickness. You all can do just as you please, but as for myself, I'll be d——d if I don't intend to ride that horse back home." Good-bye. I go from here to Wales—thence to Ireland.

Truly your friend,
H. W. A.

LETTER NO. II.

Belfast, Ireland, *July* 20, 1859.

Editors Advocate :

I wrote you a few days since, and gave the letter to a friend who sailed yesterday on the Persia. I hope the letter has gone safe to hand, and that you will have received it before this reaches you. When I wrote you I was on my way from Liverpool to Dublin. I stopped in Wales for two days, and had a very pleasant time. On the border of Wales, near the old town of Chester, is situated Eaton Hall, the seat of the Marquis of Westminster, the richest man in the British empire, his revenue being the snug little sum of $2,000,000 per annum! This estate of Eaton Hall is the most magnificent I ever saw, and completely throws into the shade every thing of the kind in our country. The residence is built after the Gothic style, is four stories high, and 500 feet in length. It is finished in the most costly and elaborate manner, and is elegantly furnished. The hot-houses, conservatories, and pleasure-gardens, are very extensive, while a park, filled with deer, extends for miles around in every direction. The noble oaks here are almost objects of veneration. They are very aged, and carry you back to the days of the Druids, whose dark and bloody rites were no doubt often celebrated on this estate. The beautiful river Dee passes through Eaton Hall, and is spanned by many iron bridges, of most airy and elegant construction, each costing a small fortune. On this large estate live about one thousand tenants. Their houses are well built, and they all appear happy, thrifty, and contented. Thus far I have travelled much through England, Wales, and Ireland, but have seen nothing like the princely establishment of Eaton Hall. It is very properly called the Paradise of the "Vale Royal of England." From Chester I passed on through Wales, and stopped a while at Bangor, to see the celebrated tubular bridge across the Menai Straits. This is certainly the king of all bridges, and is well worth seeing. It is 1500 feet long, and is supported by only two arches, the spans being 432 feet long. This, which is considered to be the triumph of the art of bridge-building, is shaped precisely like a long train of railroad cars, and made of common boiler-iron, riveted together with two millions of rivets! The cars pass through heavily loaded, and at full speed. From Bangor I passed on to Holyhead, thence across the Channel to Dublin, or rather first to Kingston, the seaport for Dublin, and thence by rail (six miles) to the great Irish capital. Dublin is a monster city, and of great antiquity. It is the Dabh-linn (black pool) of the ancient Irish, and the Eblana of Ptolemy. Here one hears the " rich Irish brogue " in all its beauty, and sees Ireland as she is at home. It has been well said that Dublin is " a faded corporation," for I saw no evidences of improvement of any kind. I spent three days in the city, and was riding round in an Irish car all the time sight-seeing, and I could only find one new house building, and that was a nunnery. Still this is a great city, and has many elegant if not magnificent buildings; all, however, bear the marks of time. St. Patrick's Cathedral is an object of great curiosity, for here lie the bones of Dean Swift. It is a splendid specimen of old Gothic art, but is surrounded by squalid wretchedness and ragged vice. It really seems to be the centre of the " five points " of Dublin. I have never in all my life seen so many old clothes, old shoes, and old hats, offered for sale, as are to be found on every street surrounding St. Patrick's Cathedral. Dean Swift was a great man in his day. In his Drapier Letters, and numerous political tracts, he defended the Irish with great zeal and ability, but was doubtless actuated more by his hatred for the English than love for the Irish. His memory is deeply revered by every Irishman, and his grave is visited almost daily by hundreds from all parts of the world. As I stood by the cold marble which marks his burial place, I thought of the devoted, the ill-requited Vanessa, the constant but unhappy Stella. I thought of Dryden and of Pope, of Addison and Steel, of Bolingbroke and Gay, all of whom paid court to the mighty Dean, and thought it an honor to be considered his friend. Swift died a wretched death. He outlived his greatness, and became a drivelling idiot. He made a strange will.

> "He gave the little wealth he had
> To build a house for fools and mad;
> And showed by one satiric touch
> No nation wanted it so much."

The river Liffey, so much boasted of by patriotic Irishmen, is a small affair, not as large as the Bayou Grosse-tête, while the celebrated College Green is nothing to compare to our Jackson Square in New Orleans. Trinity College bears much evidence of antiquity. It is the Alma Mater of nearly all the great men of Ireland, and is looked on with much pride and veneration. In point of grandeur, size and elegance, Cambridge, Yale, and the University of Virginia, are all far ahead of it. It has, however, fourteen hundred students, many of whom are Americans. In the large and spacious Catholic Cemetery, I found the graves of Curran and O'Connell—the one the great lawyer, the other the great orator. To O'Connell has been erected a splendid monument of granite, that towers proudly above all the rest, and stands in its solitary grandeur without any inscription whatever. It was built by the masses of the Irish people, each giving a few pennies apiece. Dublin has but few works of high art. In Sackville street (its Broadway) is a monument and statue to Lord Nelson, and in the churches are a few fine pieces of painting and statuary. The Phœnix Park and Botanic Gardens are perhaps the greatest curiosities. They are well kept, and are deservedly the pride of the city. Dublin has a population of about 300,000 inhabitants, and is the seat of the political, ecclesiastical, and educational institutions of Ireland. It contains seven friaries, three convents, and nine nunneries. The river Liffey divides the city almost in its centre. On Sackville street, on the road to Phœnix Park, you pass a large number of miserable mud hovels, with thatched roofs, which look as if they had been built by St. Patrick himself, immediately after he had killed all the snakes and frogs of the "Emerald Island." The whole country here is arming, the militia is training, and all seem to be on the look-out for Napoleon. I saw 10,000 militia going through their evolutions in the Park. They are fine, stout, big-boned looking men, and are officered by the nobility of the land. This is the true secret of that great success which attends the British arms the wide world over. The titled lords and gentlemen of wealth are the officers of the army and navy, and in every great battle they lead their men. They fight like Nelson for victory or Westminster Abbey. While in Dublin I visited the manufactory of the poplins, that beautiful tissue of wool and silk which makes up those lovely dresses, and runs the ladies all crazy with delight. On leaving Dublin, I passed by the Hill of Howth, through the counties of Meath, Louth and Down, to this city of Belfast. We stopped an hour or two at Drogheda, and visited the field on which was fought the "great battle of the Boyne," where William III. met James II., and, in Western language, completely "wore him out." Perhaps no battle in ancient or modern times was ever so hallowed as this battle of the Boyne, by the Protestants of Ireland. Numerous ballads have been written, generally couched in the exulting or braggadocio style, which, when sung in the presence of the Irish Catholic, invariably stirs his blood to madness, and rushes him with deadly violence upon his Orange foe. Near Drogheda, in the county of Meath, is the seat of the ancient Halls of Tara. At present nothing is left save a few melancholy ruins, to show the spot so celebrated in poetry and in song. The hill of Tara was the ancient seat of the Irish monarchs when Ireland was free, and her harp sent forth the soul of music. Her sweet bard has but too truly portrayed the deep melancholy which now surrounds that deserted spot.

"The harp that once through Tara's halls
  The soul of music shed,
Now hangs as mute on Tara's walls
  As if that soul had fled.
So sleeps the pride of former days,
  So glory's thrill is o'er;
And hearts that once beat high for praise
  Now feel that pulse no more."

Adieu, my dear sirs, 'tis late at night, and I am tired. I go to-morrow to the Giants' Causeway, and back again to this place, thence to Glasgow, Scotland.

Your friend,
H. W. A.

LETTER NO. III.

GLASGOW, SCOTLAND, *July* 23, 1859.

EDITORS ADVOCATE:

I arrived here to-day, and take this earliest opportunity to write you. In my last letter I did not have time or space to tell you of Belfast. It is the most growing city of Ireland, and already is next to Dublin in point of wealth and population. Belfast has a population of nearly 200,000 inhabitants, and is a well-built, neat, and thriving place. This is the centre of the linen trade. In the suburbs of the city are large manufactories, where those pure and spotless linens are made, which delight to cover the well-turned limbs of " God's fairest creatures." For many a mile along the railway you see acres of linens bleaching upon the smooth green sward. The city of Belfast is mostly inhabited by Protestants, who seem to hate their Catholic countrymen with " a holy hatred." Until this year, the anniversary of the battle of the Boyne, the 2d day of July, witnessed many a bloody nose and broken head.

Orangemen and Catholics met in deadly feud, and
"d——d each other's eyes," and beat each other's
heads with sticks and stones, till overpowered by
the police, backed by the militia. In consequence,
however, of a great religious revival going on now
in all the North of Ireland, these disgraceful fights
have been suspended. The day I arrived in Belfast
I attended a "street-preaching," where I found a
large assemblage, mostly of laboring men and women, who seemed to pay great attention to the minister. All of a sudden, a full-grown, athletic man
would fall down as if in spasms. His friends would
assemble around him, and bear him off amid the
soul-stirring appeals and solemn warnings of the
man of God. I heard no shoutings, or other noisy
demonstrations under religious excitement. All
was as quiet and still as the Court of Death. I
have witnessed many a camp-meeting among our
Methodist friends, where all is generally bustle and
excitement, where the screams of frightened women
are mingled with the prayers of a dozen preachers,
all addressing the throne of grace at one and the
same time. The "field-preaching" in Belfast was
altogether different, and seemed to be blessed with
great good. If it will do no other good but tame
the savage spirit of the "wild Irishman," and make
him quit the grog-shop, thousands of wives and
children will bless the good men who have preached
the word of God among them. From Belfast to
Giants' Causeway is a short distance through the
county of Antrim. At the termination of the rail-

way you take a carriage, and after a drive of five miles you reach the celebrated Causeway. The coast here is distinguished by curious and magnificent basaltic cliffs and caves. The Causeway is a platform projecting into the sea from the base of a stratified cliff 400 feet in height, and resembles a pier 700 feet in length, and 350 feet in breadth. There are about 40,000 perfectly-formed, closely-united, dark-colored polygonal columns, mostly pentagons. Their depth below the surface has never been ascertained. The popular legend says that this is the work of a giant race, seeking to construct a road to Scotland across the sea. To the geologist this formation is very interesting, and shows how symmetrical nature is in all her works. The columns are placed as close together as man could possibly place them; they will average from twelve to eighteen inches in diameter, and are perfect pentagons and hexagons. The whole are of dark basaltic rock, and are evidently of volcanic formation. After leaving the Causeway, the same basaltic formation is seen for miles on the sea-coast, one of which, a perpendicular bluff of many hundred feet in height, resembles in some degree the organ of a huge cathedral; the basaltic columns resembling in a remarkable manner the pipes of an immense organ. It was here that a huge ship belonging to the "invincible Armada" in the reign of Queen Elizabeth, in passing along the Irish coast, mistook this "basaltic organ" for a castle, and fired into it "full many an iron messenger of death." The balls of course did no damage, save the breaking of a few magnificent natural columns. History tells us that the ship ran aground near the Causeway; was taken possession of next day by the Irish, and on board they found a splendid organ, which was sent to London, and is now placed in Westminster Abbey, as a lasting monument to the folly and presumption of the Spaniards in attempting to conquer the "mistress of the seas." The Giants' Causeway being one of the great wonders of the world, is of course visited by every traveller, who brings away his pockets full of rocks, and often his hat "full of bricks," as the Irish whiskey is remarkably good in that particular latitude. For many miles back from the coast there is no timber, consequently the whole Irish coast, like Wales, presents rather a dreary appearance. The soil, however, is very rich, and produces the cereals to great perfection. In fact, the lands of Ireland are generally far superior to those of England and Scotland. Back again to Belfast (forty-five miles), where we took steamer for this city. From Belfast to Glasgow, across the Irish Sea, is about twelve hours' run. On our route we had many incidents to amuse us, and furnish much food for conversation. A large number of Scotch Presbyterian ministers were on board, returning home from their religious labors at the revival meetings in Belfast. After supper we were generally seated around the table, some reading, some talking, and others puffing the "intoxicating weed," when one of the clergymen approached us, and asked if we had any objection to their holding prayers on the steamer. Most of us of course said we had no objection. In fact, all, I believe, assented, but one man, a square-built, short-necked, pop-eyed individual, who got up out of his chair, and said "that he objected to having any such d——d nonsense where he was." An aged clergyman, sitting by me, raised his hands in horror at this seeming blasphemy. Said he to me, "My God! did you hear that, sir? I wonder that the Lord does not send a storm upon the sea and drown every one of us." And then the old man would get up, and in agony of soul walk the steamer, muttering all the while inaudible prayers. The captain was sent for, who, after talking a while to our bullet-necked, pop-eyed friend, prevailed upon him to withdraw his objections, but he could not be persuaded to remain to prayers. He stalked out of the cabin with rude violence, and his loud and long curses had scarcely died away, when our aged minister opened the lids of the sacred volume, and commenced the exercises of evening prayer. Good-bye. I shall write again soon.

Your friend,
H. W.

LETTER NO. IV.

"Ye banks and braes o' bonnie Doon,
   How can ye bloom sae fresh and fair?
How can ye chant, ye little birds,
   And I so weary, fu' o' care?
Thou'lt break my heart, thou warbling bird,
   That wantons through the flowering thorn
Thou minds me o' departed joys—
   Departed—never to return."

BONNIE DOON, SCOTLAND, *July* 25, 1859.

EDITORS ADVOCATE:

I wrote you a few days ago from Glasgow, since which time I have travelled through many important places in Scotland, and last night slept at this place, the "Burns Arms Inn," situated at the immediate spot where the great poet was born. I arrived at the village of Ayr on yesterday, and walked out to the Bonnie Doon, along whose "banks and braes" I spent the evening in sweet meditation. It was here that Burns wrote many of his best pieces. His Tam O'Shanter is generally considered one of his very best, and will live as long as his native hills endure, or the English language exists. In the Burns monument here are two very good statues, one of Tam O'Shanter, and the other of Souter Johnny, by Thom. These are lifelike, and represent Tam a few moments before he takes his celebrated ride, in the very height of his enjoyment,

> "O'er all the ills of life victorious."

The old Kirk Alloway looks as if it were still full of *bogles*, while the same stone bridge across the Doon is yet standing, and the very spot (its centre) is marked where Maggie lost her tail by the fierce grip of "Cutty Sark." Bonnie Doon is a small concern about the size of Thompson's Creek in West Feliciana. It runs through a charming country, and is decidedly the most poetic stream I have yet seen. Ayrshire is renowned for its iron works and fine cattle. Here every inch of ground is under the highest state of cultivation, while the red flames from the iron furnaces give the surrounding country a most picturesque appearance. In Burns' day, his Highland Mary may have been very pretty for all I know, but I have not seen a pretty woman yet in Scotland. They all have red hair, high cheek-bones, and freckled faces. The women here work in the fields, plough, hoe, and do all kinds of manual labor. They work twelve hours a day, from six to six, and get only a shilling, that is, twenty-four cents in our money. Still they appear happy and contented. I notice that the farmers work these women in their fields generally in gangs of fifteen or twenty, with a tall, stout Scotchman as overseer, who walks among them, and occasionally stirs them up. The Scotch farmers are very celebrated for their great knowledge of agriculture, and untiring perseverance. Their land is much poorer than that of Ireland, but they are much more successful farmers, and live much better than the Irish. I saw to-day a splendid lot of Ayrshire cows; they are not so large as the Devon and Durham, but are better milkers. From here I shall return to Glasgow, thence to Loch Lomond and the Highlands of Scotland. Glasgow is a great city, the second in the United Kingdom in many things, and the first in ship-building. It contains over 400,000 inhabitants, and is now the most thriving place in Scotland, or perhaps in all Europe. Here all the Cunard steamers are built, and here are manufactured immense quantities of Scotch woollen goods, plaids, tweeds, &c. This is the best place for building steamships in the world, as a Glasgow ship is considered the safest.

The city is situated very beautifully on the banks of the Clyde. The scenery on this river is charming. It is about as wide as the Ohio until you reach Dumbarton, where it begins to narrow, and the higher you go the smaller it becomes, until you arrive at Glasgow, when it is a very small stream, scarcely large enough for a steamer to turn round. In reading the Scottish Chiefs, you will remember what terrible deeds were done at Dumbarton. There Bruce performed prodigies of valor.

It is a round, rugged rock, separated from the mainland, and lifts its head many hundred feet above the waters of the Leven and the Clyde, which make their confluence here. For a thousand years it has been considered a stronghold, and has passed successively into the hands of Baliol, Bruce, Queen Mary, Charles I., and Cromwell. As our noble steamer, the Leopard, passed by, I felt as if the spirits of the mighty dead were still hovering around this "dreadful fortress," so often drenched with human gore. The captain of the steamer, a kind-hearted, bluff sailor, pointed out every object of interest as we passed along. In fact, I find the people here all very kind and attentive to Americans. They esteem us very highly, and claim us as kinsfolk, and in the event of a war with France, they count upon us to help them out. As we passed up the beautiful Clyde, the captain called out to me, "Do you see that tall rock just above Dumbarton?" "Yes," said I; "what is it called?" He replied, "That is the sister of Dumbarton, and is called Dumbeck." My friend, Dr. Smith, gave a broad smile, which our Scotch captain fully reciprocated. Glasgow has many elegant buildings, and much fine statuary. At every cross-road and public square are bronze figures of Scotland's most eminent men. The University of Glasgow is a magnificent building. This institution is well sustained, and stands second only to that of Edinboro'. In one of its numerous halls I noticed a fine gallery of paintings, some by those old masters, Titian and

Guido, Domenichino and Reubens. These paintings are originals, and appear to have been well selected. The Museum of Geology and Mineralogy, attached to the University, is doubtless the best in Scotland. The specimens are well arranged and classified, and must afford the student of natural science rare chances for study and improvement. While in Glasgow, I visited the spot on which formerly stood the celebrated Tolbooth. To me it was a classic place, and full of intense interest. While there I was involuntarily carried back to the days of Rob Roy McGregor and his facetious cousin, the Baillie Nicol Jarvie—to Dougal the turnkey, and young Mr. Osbaldistone. Alas! the McGregor no more stands upon his native heath, the good Baillie will never enter his favorite saut-market again. The red-headed Dougal sleeps with his Highland fathers, while no doubt the spirits of master Osbaldistone and Diana Vernon are now in close communion in other climes. I am travelling in company with Dr. S. A. Smith of Rapides. I find him a very intelligent and agreeable companion. He is a good historian, with a very retentive memory, and has been of much service to me in our travels. We are having a delightful time, intermingled frequently with fun and frolic. I hope that the good people of our State will escape our annual scourge, and that good health and general prosperity may bless them. Adieu. I shall write you from Loch Katrine. England, Scotland, and Ireland, are all arming for the great contest which they imagine must sooner or later take place between the Saxon and the Gaul. In every direction the drum and fife are heard. Around the peasant's fireside and in the palace hall, "the war with France" is the great topic of discussion. Happy America! May she always follow the good advice of Washington, and make no entangling alliances.

Yours truly,
H. W. A.

LETTER NO. V.

Clarendon Hotel, Edinboro', Scotland,
August 1, 1859.

Editors Advocate:

I believe I wrote you last from "Bonnie Doon," since which time I have travelled much by railroad, stage, and steamer " o'er the hills and far awa,'" until I have "pulled up" for a resting spell at this " Western Athens," which is full of metaphysics and oatmeal porridge, of quarterly Reviews and Scotch whiskey. This great city is the capital of Mid-Lothian, and is the metropolis of Scotland. It stands in latitude 60°, and is consequently rather a *chilly* place in the month of December. The city is built on three parallel ridges of considerable elevation. The houses are made of a beautiful white freestone, obtained from quarries near the city, and are remarkably handsome. The ridge or elevation on which the old town is built, is much higher and more abrupt than the new town, consequently the city has a very picturesque appearance. The valley between the towns was formerly filled with water, and was called the North Loch. It is now, however, a delightful place. The water is all drained off, and it is principally used as an aristocratic park, where the children and nurses of the nobility and gentry of Edinboro' repair to " air " themselves, for the ragged mob and barelegged loafers are kept out by bars and bolts and sturdy policemen. In Edinboro' a hard-working mechanic with his freckled-faced son, can it is true, go to the top of Arthur's Seat, and feast his eyes on the beauties of this great city. He can then descend and go to the base of Sir Walter's monument, and look with pleasure and with pride on Scotland's greatest man; but let him attempt to enter this iron-grated aristocratic park, and he would be kicked out with as little ceremony as a negro would be from a public ball-room in Baton Rouge. This is not in population a great city, as compared with London, or Paris, or Vienna; but in literature, in the arts, in medicine, in law, philosophy, and the natural sciences, in poetry and in song, and above all in literary periodicals, Edinboro' stands pre-eminently ahead of all the civilized world. In the long list of immortal names that have been written on the scroll of fame, Scotia claims her full portion, and more, perhaps, than any other nation. Wallace and Bruce, Scott and Burns, and Allan Ramsay, Dugald Stewart, Reid and Playfair, Knox, Brown, and Chalmers, Hume, Mackintosh, and Robertson, are names that will live " till the last syllable of recorded time." It is indeed a matter of great astonishment that Scotland, a small, hilly, poor, rugged country, should have given so many great men to the world. Edinboro' has a population of 160,000 inhabitants; about the size of Cincinnati. It is very pleasantly situated near the Frith of Forth, and is now accessible by railroads from all quarters. To a stranger, this city presents many strange sights—the buildings frequently towering up to the height of eight or ten stories, while the railway passes over the tops of houses, and you seem really to be travelling on *an air line*. The principal streets in the old town, and the ones known to history and to fame, are Canongate and High street. This street (for they both are the same) is a mile long, and rises gradually from Holyrood Palace, with a regular and steep inclination, until it terminates in the huge rock on which is built the castle, 443 feet above the level of the sea. It was on this street that the celebrated John Knox lived. His house is still standing, and the window is pointed out, from which he thundered forth his terrible anathemas against the follies and the wickedness of the times. He was no temporizing, milk-and-cider, cream-cheese preacher. He spared neither king nor queen, priest nor people, but boldly lashed vice wherever found, in pampered wealth or squalid poverty. He cried aloud and spared not. Elegance of rhetoric and delicacy of language were not common in his time, and would have been lost in the tumult. He spoke and wrote his honest thoughts in terse and even homely language. He appeared in the pulpit not in the graceful folds of the toga, or the simple and unpretending dress of a reforming clergyman, but he came as a warrior, clad in mail, armed at all points, for defence and aggression. He was inflexible in maintaining what he felt to be right, and intrepid in defending it. On his death he was buried in the churchyard of St. Giles, and his eulogist pronounced these memorable words—" Here lies he who never feared the face of man." The most remarkable place in Edinboro' is of course the castle. It is situated on the top of a high rock, and is a cluster of irregular buildings, begirt with embrazured walls, except on the south side, where the castle rises perpendicularly with the rock, which it emulates in sternness of aspect and lofty grandeur. From a window on this portion of the castle you have the best prospect in Scotland. Just under you is the celebrated " Grass Market," and many of the most busy thoroughfares of the city, while opposite rise in all their majesty Salisbury Crags and Arthur's Seat.

The fortress contains generally a small number of soldiers. It has accommodations for 2,000, and the armory for 30,000 stand of arms. I saw here a huge cannon made of malleable iron; its bore is two feet six inches in diameter, and ought to carry a ball about the size of a flour-barrel! This monster gun was made in Mons, in Belgium, A. D. 1486. The castle contains a great many articles of curiosity and a number of historic apartments. Here James VI. was born. Here Queen Mary was confined. Here are the regalia of Scotland, the sceptre, crown, and sword. Here also are the instruments of torture, used in the days of Charles and of James; the thumb-screw and the iron boot, the wheel and the rack, melancholy mementos of the dreadful persecutions of the Covenanters. The Palace of Holyrood, or Holyrood House, is situated at the lower or eastern extremity of Canongate street. It is a huge, square building, with an open central court about 100 feet square. In the north-west angle of the palace are the apartments of Mary Queen of Scots, nearly in the same state as when left by that unfortunate princess. The furniture looks old and rickety, and the beds and bedding, and fancy curtains, and regal trappings, are all faded and worm-eaten. It is here in this very room that the spots of blood on the floor are shown the visitor, it being the place where the hapless Rizzio was murdered in the very presence of his mistress. Adjoining the palace, on the north side, is the chapel in which Queen Mary was married to Lord Darnley. Here are deposited the remains of many of the kings and noble personages of Scotland. This old palace is fitted up at present, or rather a suite of rooms has been fitted up, for the express benefit of his Highness the Prince of Wales, who now resides here, and is studying chemistry at the University. He is an ordinary-looking youth, of modest demeanor and agreeable manners. Edinboro' is all agog because he has come here to attend the University. He puts on no airs, but goes about the city in a plain and unpretending manner. There are 23 churches here, of what is called the "Established Church." Among them the finest are St. George's, St. Stephen's, St. Mary's, and St. Andrew's. Of the Free churches there are 25. There are 15 United Presbyterian and 8 Episcopalian churches. St. John's in Prince's street and St. George's in York place are elegant structures. There are also in the city 6 Baptist, 3 Methodist, 3 Congregational, 2 Seceders, 1 Reformed Presbyterian, and 2 Roman Catholic churches. The Greyfriars churchyard attached to the old Greyfriars church, is one of the most interesting spots in Scotland. Here lie buried Sir George Mackenzie, Allan Ramsay the poet, and Robertson the historian. In this churchyard also are buried many who suffered martyrdom in the times of the persecution, and here it was on the top of the tombstones, over the sacred graves of their fathers, that the national covenant was signed in 1638. In the way of monuments Edinboro' has some splendid specimens. The most elegant is that erected to Sir Walter Scott, on Prince's street. It is a Gothic cross, 200 feet high. A statue, in sitting posture, of the great poet and novelist, occupies the platform of the monument, and over it the groined arches form a canopy. This structure is in most excellent taste, and is one of the most beautiful specimens of "monumental art" I have ever seen.

On Carlton Hill are many other monuments. The national monument, begun for those who fell at Waterloo, was intended to be a literal reproduction of the Parthenon, but for want of funds its progress has been arrested. Only a few columns have been erected, and now Carlton Hill has somewhat the appearance of the ruins of the Acropolis of Athens. On this hill are the monuments to Nelson, Dugald Stewart, and Playfair. The University here is the best in Scotland, and second to none in Europe. The buildings are large and spacious, with an open court in the centre. The library contains 100,000 volumes. There are usually 1200 students in attendance, taught by 32 professors, in law, medicine, divinity, and the arts. The legitimate expenses of a student here for board and tuition, are about four hundred dollars per year. The sons of the nobility and gentry, however, spend a great deal more. I examined this matter particularly, and found that our youth at the University of Virginia, or Cambridge, or Princeton, spend more money than do the students at the University of Edinboro'. In the first place, the habits of Americans are much more liberal—they make their money faster and easier, and spend it with an open hand. In this city the hotels are well kept, but they charge most extravagant prices. All are kept in the restaurant style. They charge in the bill, for soap and candles, and for every dish ordered, and then the waiter's fee is included; notwithstanding all this, the well-dressed, portly-looking *white servant* comes up with cap in hand, and begs you to *remember* him.

When I wrote you last I was in "Bonnie Doon." I went back to Glasgow; took rail and then down to Dumbarton; thence out to Loch Lomond; up this Loch to Inversnaid, where we staid all night, at the foot of Ben Lomond, whose tall and rugged head was ever under a cloud. On Sunday morning we took stage and passed over to Loch Katrine, a distance of only five or six miles. Here we took a sail-boat and went up Loch Katrine to the Trosachs, where we rested for the evening. Next morning, by stage again to Calender, some eight or ten miles, where we took rail and proceeded by the "Bridge of Allan" (a celebrated watering-place) to Stirling, thence by Bannockburn to Edinboro'. In this short journey how many names appear which have become classic in the history of this country! Dumbarton, Stirling Castle, and Bannockburn! These are names that must emblazon Scottish history forever. Lochs Lomond and Katrine are beautiful sheets of water, interspersed with romantic islands. In the "Lady of the Lake," I do not think that Sir Walter Scott has overdrawn the picture. The mountain scenery is peculiarly soft, for the very top of Ben Lomond is covered with green mosses, or lichens, which hide those ragged cliffs and rugged rocks that are seen in higher mountains. In going from Lomond to Katrine, we passed the "muster-place of Lanrick Mead," and entered upon the grounds of Roderick

Dhu. Close at hand is Fitz James's rock, on which the monarch stood, when

> "The maid alarmed, with hasty oar
> Pushed her light shallop from the shore,
> Then safe, though fluttered and amazed,
> She paused, and on the stranger gazed;
> Not his the form or his the eye
> That youthful maidens wont to fly."

The island on which the Douglass entertained Fitz James, is shown the traveller. It is called "Ellen's Isle," and is a small, rugged, rocky affair, grown over with bushes, "with brier and with brake." Little does it look now, as if the Douglass ever held court there, but the "Lady of the Lake" says so, and we are bound to believe *her*. The Trosachs is the place where the royal hunter lost the stag. It was here that this

> "Wily quarry shunned the shock,
> And turned him from the opposing rock;
> Then dashing down a darksome glen,
> Soon lost to hound and hunter's ken,
> In the deep Trosachs' wildest nook
> His solitary refuge took."

To the lover of poetry and of song—to one who has read with interest the "Lady of the Lake," which, taken all together, is the most chaste and elegant poem ever written, the mountain scenery of Scotland is perfectly enchanting. The lovely Loch Katrine is the most beautiful sheet of water I ever saw. In order to view this lake in its most poetic aspect, I took the path that had been taken by Fitz James, and gained a far projecting precipice. It was about the time for the setting sun, and Loch Katrine lay before me

> "One burnished sheet of living gold."

I lingered till a late hour of the night, and as I took my solitary way back to the Trosachs Hotel, my brain was filled with a thousand thick-coming fancies. As I passed along, methought I met the henchman Malise "speeding on his warlike mission," with burning brand. On the roadside lay "Red Murdock stiff and stark;" farther on I heard the shrill whistle of Roderick Dhu, and

> "Instant from heath and copse arose
> Bonnets and spears and bended bows."

When the Waverly Novels were written, Loch Katrine and its surroundings must have been exceedingly wild and romantic—much more so than at present, for as civilization advances, railroads are built, huge hotels are erected, and the mob, the world and his wife, and everybody else, travel and desecrate those sacred spots that should be reserved for the true lovers of nature. The people of Glasgow have tapped this beautiful Loch Katrine, and are now taking its pure and delicious waters a distance of thirty-five or forty miles, to quench the thirst of the red-headed, gin-drinking, overworked operatives of that great manufacturing city. Calender is quite a pretty place, and reminds you very much of the villages in the valley of Virginia. Here the rails begin, and the face of the country gets smooth and well-cultivated, for in the mountains around Loch Lomond and Loch Katrine there is no such thing as a field, or even a habitation. It is all wild mountains, covered with heather, supporting only a few black-faced sheep. I regret that I have not time to tell you of the cottage in which the MacGregor was born. It is close to the roadside, and not far from Inversnaid. I should also wish to say something of "Stirling Castle." When I beheld the towers of this ancient fortress, oh, what mournful recollections rushed upon my mind! Here are still kept

> "The wheel and axe, and headsman's sword,
> And many an hideous engine grim
> For wrenching joint and crushing limb."

It was in this castle, "through grated arch and passage dread," that old Allan-bane was led, when he visited the sick couch of Clan Alpine's chief, and sang that mournful dirge which caused the mighty heart of Roderick Dhu to break. The town of Stirling is quite a place. It has a population of about 14,000 inhabitants, and is the favorite residence of many of the most noble and ancient families of Scotland. It is situated on the right bank of the Forth, and is 30 miles by rail from Edinboro'. A few miles from Stirling, immediately on the road, is the village of Bannockburn, situated pleasantly on the Bannock, a small stream flowing into the Frith. Here it was that Bruce, with his gallant Scots, met the English under Edward II., on the 24th June, 1314. It derives its name from the oaten cakes or bannocks made in the mills on its banks. The English were defeated with great slaughter, for there was no retreat, but a blind rout and helpless flight. Burns has immortalized this battle by his celebrated national song, and here stands a noble monument erected to Scotland's greatest man, the " Bruce of Bannockburn." This evening I visited the Salisbury Crags, and the top of Arthur's Seat. Here is a charming prospect in view. On the right sleeps the calm and gentle Frith of Forth. On the left stretch out as far as the eye can reach the Pentland Hills; immediately in front is the beautiful city of Edinboro', with its parks, its towers and steeples. There, in that old rickety house, lived Jennie Deans, the amiable, the kind, the pious Jennie. There is the " Grass Market," that dark and bloody ground, where many a Presbyterian and Covenanter received the martyr's crown. Dunedin, adieu! Thy shame and thy glory stand recorded on the pages of never-dying history.

Yours, truly,
H. W. A.

LETTER NO. VI.

TRAFALGAR HOTEL, LONDON, ENGLAND,
August 6, 1859.

EDITORS ADVOCATE:

I arrived in this "great Babel" some four or five days since, and have put up at the Trafalgar Hotel, near the monument and close to the Spring Gardens. I find my hotel a very quiet and agreeable place. My travelling companion, Dr. Smith, is still in the north of Scotland, among the "kilts and tartans," for which he seems to have taken quite a fancy. Shelby and Johnson are, however, with me, two glorious Mississippians. We occasionally get on a "burst," and astonish these phlegmatic Englishmen very much indeed. On our arrival here, after registering our names, we proceeded to take a glass of ale, and then went—to take another glass of ale, when Shelby told the following story: "Once upon a time, the Governor of South Carolina met the Governor of North Carolina, and says the Governor of South Carolina to the Governor of North Carolina, 'Governor, it is a d—d long time between drinks;' whereupon the Governor of North Carolina said to the Governor of South Carolina, 'Governor, suppose we *do take* a drink!'" on which Johnson proposed that we should all take a drink. Now be it remembered we had just arrived from Edinboro'. This was our first night in London, and we wanted to see the town; so after taking a turn up the Hay Market for a short distance, we called a carriage, and told the Britisher to drive us to the "Comorn Gardens." In due course of time we arrived, and found them crowded with beauty and fashion, with old age and ugliness; with very lean people and very fat people. These gardens are gotten up on a most magnificent scale, after the Parisian style. They cover several acres of ground, and contain dancing saloons, fairy cottages, artificial grottos, and many other places to amuse the fancy and "delight the heels" of the seekers of pleasure. I think there must have been, at the lowest calculation, 10,000 persons at these gardens. The music is very fine, and the gas-lights most artistically and beautifully arranged. The "Vaux Hall" Gardens in former days were all the rage, and their brilliancy often astonished "the country bumpkins" who came up to London. These have passed away, and now the "Comorn" have opened with transcendent splendor. Of course the *élite* of the city seldom visit this place; it seems to be mostly frequented by the fast young men and women of London, who come here to dance to delicious music, and pass an hour or two in the "little frivolities" of life. Admission one shilling—children half price—no negroes here. By the by, you very seldom see a negro in Great Britain, except at Liverpool, where there are a good many sailors. When Daniel Webster arrived in London, he said to his cab-driver, "Take me to the Tower." Now I differed from the great Daniel, for the morning after I arrived I told my Jehu to drive me to the House of Lords. I wanted to see the acting, living, great men of the world; the men who governed Parliament, and through Parliament the world. A fig for your Tower and its ancient renown and worm-eaten glory! On entering the House of Lords, I found the Chief Justice on the woolsack, with huge wig and black gown. On his right sat Henry Lord Brougham; on his left another distinguished Lord. They were trying an appeal case, and the counsel addressing them I thought was particularly heavy and dry. Brougham looks hearty and hale, although 80 years old. He resembles in a remarkable degree, John Bell of Tennessee, and Judge Moore of St. Martin, Louisiana. I asked a policeman, a stout, well-dressed beef-eater, to point out to me Lord Brougham. His reply was, "Have you never seen his portraits? He is exactly like his portraits." Said I, "No sir, I never saw his portraits." "Great God," said the policeman, "where have you been all your life?" To which I modestly replied, that I had been all my life in the United States, where we considered Lord Brougham a small concern, and didn't care a d—n for him or his portraits. On this we played quits; the "man of authority" gazing at me as if I were a savage from the wild woods of North America. The chamber of the House of Lords is elegantly fitted up with all the luxury of modern art. Like the House of Commons, the Lords sit on benches and not in chairs. The woolsack is a crimson-covered sack, or more like a square bed, on which the Lord Chancellor sits. The position must be very uncomfortable, for there is no support for the back. They should therefore select for this honored post the man who has the *strongest backbone*. The chamber is badly arranged; the spectators' gallery very small, and the whole affair seemingly much contracted. The trappings of royalty are fully carried out here. All the officers, sergeants-at-arms, and door-keepers are in full uniform, with long swords at their sides. While in London I visited the House of Lords frequently, and witnessed the debates. I was anxious to hear Lord Macaulay, but he was in very bad health. The Duke of Argyle, a small, red-headed man, about 40 years of age, seemed to be the most active business man in the House. He married the daughter of the Duchess of Sutherland, and is now the proprietor of immense estates. In this aristocratic assembly there are now but few great statesmen or orators. Brougham is failing fast—is now almost in his dotage, and his place cannot be well supplied. Macaulay will soon die, for he has softening of the brain. Argyle is a man of education, but lacks genius. The Lords behave themselves much better than the Commons, and only about *one-half of them* wear their hats during the sittings. Most of them are very old men, and a great majority bald-headed. They seem to doze away their time upon the benches, and occasionally wake up with the cry of "hear, hear." I also visited the House of Commons frequently. It meets only at night, and often sits till daybreak. In going into the House of Commons you pass into an anteroom filled with statuary. The first is Fox, with his huge fist doubled up in a threatening attitude; opposite is Pitt, his great and successful rival. Next is the great Lord Chatham; then Burke, and Walpole, and many others who have made their mark in the House of Commons. The arrangements for admission to strangers are exceedingly unpleasant and tiresome. The strangers' gallery holds only about 100 persons. It is generally filled. You consequently take your seat in the anteroom, and look at the cold marble statues, till your time comes, which may not be till midnight, or not at all. I found that a half-crown invariably made all right, and I was passed through every evening to a front seat. I tell you there is great virtue in a half-crown; it is about the size of our half-dollar, and looks as big to a British beef-eater as one of our saw-mill timber wheels. Having obtained ready admission to the House of Commons, I attended nearly every evening while I was in London. There is a great deal of talent in the

House. The Premier, Lord Palmerston, is a man of high order of intellect, while Lord John Russell is every inch a statesman. The Chancellor of the Exchequer, Mr. Gladstone, has no equal in Great Britain for clear and concise logic, for pure and elegant rhetoric. These are all what is called "Administration men." On the opposite or conservative side are D'Israeli and Whiteside, Roebuck and John Bright, all men of the highest order of talent, who have studied politics as a profession, and are well learned in all the branches of political economy. I do not like the style of English speaking as well as our own. Lord John gets up, for instance, and commences his speech, perfectly self-possessed, it is true, but he enunciates his words exceedingly slow, and seems to hem and haw in selecting them. He never permits himself to be excited or aroused. On one occasion, while attending the debates, I heard Mr. Maguire, the member for the University of Dublin, pitch into Lord John most terribly. He denounced him right and left, and told him that *his* government would go down to posterity with dishonor and disgrace, and that *his* name would be the by-word and contempt of future ages, because he, the said Lord John, would not use the power of the British arms against Bologna, in order to make the Italians submit to the Pope. Lord John replied in his cool and temperate manner, and completely demolished the Irishman. The Government side raised such a cry of "hear, hear, hear," that it was really ap-

palling to their adversaries. By the way, this Mr.
Maguire is a very learned man and fine scholar.
His style of speaking, his manner, his very appearance, remind you forcibly of our distinguished fellow-citizen, the Hon. Michael Ryan, of Rapides, and
in this connection I would remark that Lord John
would be taken very readily for an elder brother
of the Hon. Duncan F. Kenner, of Ascension.
They are as much alike as two black-eyed peas or
two bald-headed men possibly can be. D'Israeli
is a singular-looking man. His Jewish features
and long gray locks attract your attention immediately. His voice is good and clear, and his delivery very graceful. He stands at the head of the
Opposition in the House. John Bright is a large,
fine-looking, stout man, resembling somewhat
Toombs, of Georgia, in his personal appearance, and
his earnest and impassioned style of speaking.
The Premier, Lord Palmerston, is about six feet
one or two inches high; is a fine specimen of an
old English gentleman; dresses in gay and fancy
colors, and is the Roger de Coverley of the House.
He is almost *a century old*, but still is active in
mind and body, and as a member of Parliament
can out-sit any of the young members now. His
style of speaking is plain, and to the point. He
deals in no poetry, no figures of speech, but goes
right up and grapples with his subject in a bold
and straightforward manner, without stopping to
pick up the flowers of rhetoric. In the House of
Commons the members all sit with their hats on.

They seem to take a pride in this, for I noticed that after finishing their speeches, they, on resuming their seats, immediately put on their hats. I should think that in a warm room, in hot weather, it would be much more comfortable to sit with hats off, but there is no accounting for tastes. A Britisher prefers " a Welsh rare-bit " to the finest wild turkey stuffed with truffles! I noticed that the Speaker of the House of Commons seldom, if ever, takes what we call the " ayes and noes." When a question is to be decided, he says (holding the paper in his hand) " all who are in favor of the passage of this bill will go to the right; all who are opposed to it will go to the left." They separate immediately and retire into adjoining rooms, where tellers count the vote and report to the assembled House.

The House of Commons consists of 640 members. It is very seldom that all are present. But few men do all the work. Every thing is done in committee. The bills are all prepared there, and reported on and passed, often without debate. The members of Parliament receive no pay, consequently none but the wealthy, or those who have wealthy friends, can enter public life. The canvassing for a seat in Parliament costs frequently immense sums. Bribery and corruption then becomes common, and so offensive is it now in the nostrils of the nation, that committees are now sitting on charges of this nature against several members of the House. Already one of them has been unseated, with a fair prospect of ousting several other honorable members. Our Congress at Washington may be exceedingly disorderly at times, but I think it can compare very favorably with the House of Commons of Great Britain. They may not chew tobacco and spit on the floors as we do, but they cock up their feet, with their hats over their eyes, and are continually crying out "hear, hear, hear, hear," on the most frivolous occasions.

Westminster Abbey is just opposite to the House of Lords, and is entered by the "Poets' Corner." This Abbey is an enormous old cathedral, built at a very early day, when its peculiar Gothic architecture was much used, and carried to great perfection. This old church has become the burial-ground of England's "noblest dead," for many ages. It has nine chapels, dedicated each to a patron saint. The "Poets' Corner" is by far the most interesting part of the immense structure, for at every step you find the ashes of some great poet who has left behind him works more durable than dull cold marble. In passing along, the first striking monument is that of Joseph Addison, by Westmacott, with this inscription: "Whoever thou art, venerate the memory of Joseph Addison."

Next, over the door of the chapel of St. Blaize, is the monument of Oliver Goldsmith, M. D., by Nollekens. The inscription is, "He was master of the softer passions, and could at pleasure command tears or provoke laughter; but in every thing that he said or did, good-nature was predominant."

On the left is Gay's monument, erected by the Duke and Duchess of Queensbury. The epitaph is by himself—

> "Life is a jest, and all things show it;
> I thought so once, but now I know it."

Next are Rowe and Thomson author of The Seasons. Standing next to Thomson's is the monument to William Shakspeare. It is of good design and very elegantly finished. The great bard is represented as seated in a quiet and thoughtful manner, with a scroll in his hand, on which is written—

> "The cloud-capped towers—the gorgeous palaces—
> The solemn temples—the great globe itself—
> Yea, all which it inherits, shall dissolve,
> And like the baseless fabric of a vision,
> Leave not a wreck behind."

These are only a few of the many splendid monuments erected to England's greatest poets. Here are Campbell and Southey; Matthew Prior and Samuel Butler; Spenser and rare Ben Jonson; Chaucer and Cowley, and the ever great and glorious Milton. Under Milton is an elegant monument, erected to the memory of Gray, with this inscription:

> "No more the Grecian muse unrivalled reigns;
> To Britain let the nations homage pay:
> She felt a nation's fire in Milton's strains,
> A Pindar's rapture in the lyre of Gray."

The chapel of Henry VII. is the most gorgeous. It is filled with ancient tombs of rare workmanship. Its gates are of bronze, and the entire ceiling of curiously carved stone. Here are the remains of the haughty Elizabeth, by the side of her victim, the Queen of Scots.

In passing through the long aisles and gloomy chapels of "this cemetery of England's greatest dead," I could find no monuments to Horatio Nelson or John Bunyan. Their mortal remains do not lie here. Although Nelson's great battle-cry was "Victory or Westminster Abbey," he was denied a burial here. As to Bunyan, the poor despised son of a tinker, his grave is in some suburban churchyard, nobody knows where. It is to England's shame that these two men, who have shed more glory on her arms and religion, than any others of her long list of worthies, should have been denied a burial in Westminster Abbey. They were not unlike in their lives. Nelson was a brave sailor, a consummate admiral. He saved England in her greatest hour of danger, for he conquered Napoleon at the battle of the Nile, and crushed him at Trafalgar. Bunyan, too, was a soldier. He was at the siege of Leicester, in the Parliament army. Professing religion, he joined the Baptist church, and commenced preaching the Gospel. He was persecuted as a dissenter. He was tried, convicted, and imprisoned for twelve long years. During this whole time he "kept the faith," and here it was he wrote that work, which is now in every palace and in every cottage in Christendom. John Bunyan believed in the efficacy of prayer. So did Lord Nelson. In all his engagements, before going into battle, he knelt upon the quarter-deck of his ship, and prayed that God would give him the victory. The influence of these two men is more felt to-day, than any others who have lived or died on British soil. How often have I seen the widowed mother take her little orphans on her knees, and with the Pilgrim's Progress in her hand, tell them the interesting story of Christian—his trials and his troubles, and how at last he reached the New Jerusalem. This beautiful allegory affects the tender minds of children in an astonishing manner. It can never be eradicated. Even in after years, when far away from parents and from home, these early lessons, taught by a fond mother, come gushing up, and we involuntarily exclaim, "God bless John Bunyan. He was a good old man." His Pilgrim's Progress has softened the heart of many a wayward boy, and turned his footsteps from the paths of vice to seek the joys of Heaven at last.

Adieu. I shall write you again from this city.

Yours, truly,

H. W. A.

LETTER NO. VII.

Trafalgar Hotel, London, England,
August 9, 1859.

Editors Advocate:

I leave to-morrow for Paris, and have concluded to write you again from this place. This is a monster city. Its population, strange to say, is rapidly increasing, and now numbers three millions of inhabitants! The largest city in the world. No man can form any idea of a crowded city until he sees London. I have stood on Broadway, New York, and thought that it was utterly impossible to get together more people than generally congregate on that great thoroughfare; but take your position on the Strand in London for an hour, and you will swear that the whole world had concluded, in "English parlance," to come up to town.

My hotel on Trafalgar Square, is in a very central portion of London. It is only a few squares from the Thames, and a short walk from the Parliament House. The great artery or thoroughfare of London is the Strand. Everybody from "up town" has to go down this street, to cross London Bridge, to go to the Bank of England, or to the Post Office. You jump into an omnibus to go to the bank; you pass through the Strand, then Temple Bar, then along Fleet Street, Ludgate Hill, St. Paul's, Cheapside, Cornhill, and Leadenhall Street, all one continued street, to Threadneedle Street, on which is the mammoth Bank of England. This bank is a low, flat, insulated building, covering four acres of ground. It has a governor and deputy-governor, and a board of twenty-four directors. It commenced business on the 1st of January, 1695. From time to time the capital has been increased, until now it is $60,000,000. While in the bank they showed me a bill for £1,000,000 sterling! Money is loaned here at two-and-a-half per cent. per annum.

One of the greatest curiosities, or rather wonders of London, is the "Crystal Palace" at Sydenham. This is the celebrated palace used in London during the World's Fair. After the fair, it was pulled down, and removed to the village of Sydenham, about eight miles out of town, and put up again, but with increased dimensions, and far greater splendor. It is astonishing to see here what the art and ingenuity of man can do. The palace is an enormous structure, flanked with towers 300 feet high, on the top of which are huge cisterns. These cisterns are kept full of water by force pumps, and supply the water-works attached to the grounds. The numerous fountains scattered through the immense grounds, are most tastefully arranged. They throw up solid columns of water 280 feet high! There is nothing like it in the wide world. This Crystal Palace is about a quarter of a mile long, and is made of glass and iron. It is filled with curiosities of every conceivable kind. One portion of it is entirely filled with exotic plants, all bearing fruit. Here is the clove and the nutmeg, and the cinnamon tree. The coffee and the tea plants are growing side by side, in close familiarity with the broad-leaved sugar-cane. Here are the banana and the cocoanut; the tamarind and the banyan; the tall and stately palm and humble olive. In fact, so great is the display of exotics here, and so dense the thicket, that you fancy yourself in one of the jungles of Bengal, and almost hear the screams of the bright-plumed parrots, and the growl of the royal tiger. In this palace there is an immense theatre or concert-hall, large enough to accommodate 10,000 persons. Here I heard the charming little Piccolomini. I noticed among the other curiosities here, a California pine tree about 30 feet in diameter! The bark had been cut in sections and stripped from its trunk. It was set up again as it grew in the forest, to the height of 100 feet. The interior of this huge tree was occupied as a sitting-room.

There are also in the palace large refreshment rooms—restaurants, cake and beer stands, &c.,

&c.; for be it remembered, wherever an Englishman goes, he must have something to eat and drink. I verily believe, unless he is purified on earth, that when he gets to heaven, and finds there no "roast-beef, or potatoes, or porter and ale," that he will be a miserable man through all eternity. The surroundings of the Crystal Palace are in the same grand style of magnificence. The grounds contain some four or five hundred acres of land, and are laid off in elegant walks, artificial lakes and grottos. In these lakes I noticed huge antediluvian animals, built of brick and mortar, and made in the most accurate and artistic style, not so much for show, as for instruction to the million.

From the Crystal Palace I went on to "Hampton Court," some ten miles farther. This is the residence of the Duchess of Kent, and is considered the aristocratic poor-house of England, for here "our poor relations" are kept in style and fed in state. This is an immense old palace, with beautiful grounds attached, shaded with huge lime trees. The palace was built by Cardinal Wolsey, when he was in his "pride of power," and has been for many centuries the favorite retreat of the sovereigns of Great Britain. The proud and haughty cardinal lived here in great state. Here it was he entertained his royal master, Henry VIII., in such magnificent style; and here it was that he might have lived to the end, but "avarice and ambition" pulled him down, and made him feel "how wretched is that poor man, that hangs on princes' favors." I have often felt for poor old Wolsey. He was a " scholar, and a ripe and good one." To them that loved him not, he was "lofty and sour," but to those that sought him he was "sweet as summer." He did not, it is true, "serve his God with half the zeal he served his king," but he was liberal to a fault, and in bestowing, he was most princely. Bluff Harry certainly treated him badly, and should not have left him,

> "Weary and old with service, to the mercy
> Of a rude stream."

It was here in Hampton Court that Edward VI. was born, his mother Jane Seymour surviving his birth only a few days. This Jane Seymour is the same lady who married Henry VIII. the day after Queen Anne Boleyn had her head cut off. The royal Blue-Beard having disposed of five wives, resolved to take the sixth, and on the 12th of July, 1543, he married the Lady Catharine Parr, at Hampton Court. It was here that Queen Mary (bloody Mary) and her husband, Philip of Spain, passed their honeymoon in gloomy retirement. The immense palace has been added to, by nearly every monarch, and now covers a large space. Sir Christopher Wren built the gallery for the cartoons of Raphael. These are painted on sheets of thick paper, and are very properly esteemed the pride of the "Galleries of the Court." They represent eight scenes from the New Testament—the death of Ananias, Peter and John at the Beautiful Gate, the Miraculous Draught of Fishes, Paul and Barnabas at Lystra, &c., &c. There are many other fine paintings in the various galleries here, by Holbein and Van Dyck, and Lely and Kneller, and a host of others. The grounds attached to this palace are on a large scale; they are kept in most excellent order. In one of the gardens I noticed an immense grape-vine, 120 feet long and 3 feet in circumference. This is said to be the largest grape-vine in the world. It is the black Hamburg grape, and generally bears 2,500 bunches, of a good season.

From Hampton Court I went over to Richmond, a few miles, and spent an hour in that quiet village, visiting, among other places, Twickenham, once the residence of Pope. It is a pretty place, immediately on the banks of the Thames, and presents, even now, with all its changes, a very poetic appearance. Here the Thames becomes quite small, and this is the head of steamboat navigation.

Jumping on board the little steamer, I was in a few hours safely landed on Westminster Bridge, only a few yards from my hotel. The Thames is a narrow but a very deep river. It admits the largest class vessels up to London. Even the Great Eastern is built here, and is now nearly finished. She will be able to come up to any wharf in London, and take in her cargo. Over the Thames are eight bridges; four stone, three iron, and one wood. London Bridge is the oldest. It is built of Aberdeen granite; is 928 feet long, 53 feet wide, has five arches, and cost £2,000,000 sterling. This is the bridge from which so many persons throw themselves into the dark waters of the Thames. At London this river is about 250 yards wide. As you approach the sea, forty miles distant, it gets wider and wider, till you reach Gravesend, where it is quite a respectable stream, about the size of the Atchafalaya, where it goes into Berwick's Bay.

In my last letter, I failed to describe the new Palace of Westminster, or the House of Parliament. It is an immense pile, on the very banks of the Thames, built after the Tudor Gothic style, from designs by Sir Charles Barry. It covers an area of 8 acres, and is 900 feet in length. The walls are of brick, faced externally with limestone. The waters of the Thames wash its very foundations, which are made of Aberdeen granite. The entire building is panelled with rich tracery, and profusely decorated with statues and shields, and coats of arms of the numerous kings and queens of England. In the south-west angle is the Victoria Tower, 75 feet square and 340 feet high. This great building is magnificently decorated throughout, with carved oak panelling, gilding, fresco painting, and richly stained-glass windows. Take it all in all, and it is the finest state building in the world, and the most perfect specimen of Gothic architecture now in existence.

The Tower next claims our attention. It stands on the banks of the Thames, and occupies an area of 12 acres, not very far from London Bridge. On the south side is an archway called the "Traitor's Gate," through which state prisoners were brought from the river. Tradition says that Julius Cæsar laid the foundations of this ancient fortress, but we know that in 1078 William the Conqueror built what is called the White Tower. It stands in the quadrangle, around which are several other towers, each known by its own distinctive name. Besides its use as a fortress, the Tower has been the temporary residence of many of the royal family. But it is as a great gloomy state prison, where kings and queens, statesmen, warriors, and philosophers have been confined, that history has brought down to us the "Tower of London." In the days of the Tudors and Plantagenets, the cry was, "To the Tower," and soon the head of the unfortunate victim was seen in the fatal basket. Here Edward V. and his tender brother were smothered by order of the "bloody Richard," and here Anne Boleyn and Catharine Howard were taken to the "block of shame." In passing along the gloomy passages and dark corridors of the Tower, I thought of Queen Anne and Margaret; of Hastings and Buckingham; of Rivers, and Vaughan, and Grey, and then methought I saw flitting along, the son-in-law of renowned Warwick, the false, fleeting, perjured Clarence, and heard him in his deep anguish exclaim,

> "O God! if my deep prayers cannot appease thee,
> But thou wilt be avenged on my misdeeds;
> Yet execute thy wrath on me alone;
> Oh! spare my guiltless wife and my poor children!"

The room is shown wherein lay the royal children, "those gentle babes" so early doomed to death. In visiting this room, the tear of sympathy is often shed over the sad fate of these tender princes. In an apartment appropriated especially to the purpose, are seen the Regalia of England; the crown jewels, bracelets, brooches, &c. Here also is the celebrated "Koorinoor diamond," together with many other jewels, of lesser note, all exposed to view, under a strong iron framework, covered with glass. This apartment is kept by a *female person*, who goes through her rigmarole of stereotype descriptions in a very fast and indistinct manner, and then immediately takes her seat at the door, expecting every one to drop her a penny or two, as they pass out. The armory hall is a series of rooms appropriated to all species of weapons, from the earliest to the present date. Here are cannon and stacks of arms taken by the British in their battles all over the globe. Here are guns and pistols of every age and country. Here is the cross-bow of Robin Hood, and the claymore of Rob Roy, the Macgregor. Here also is the battle-axe of Richard the Lion-hearted, and the breast-plate and helmet of Edward the Black Prince. The swords of Cromwell, of Marlborough, of Nelson, and of Wellington, are exhibited here with great pride and ostentation by the numerous guides. These guides are dressed in full military uniform, with fancy cocked hats, ornamented with numerous bows of pink ribbon. They are selected from the commissioned officers of the army, who have become aged or wounded in the service. The post is a very lucrative one, for nearly every visitor gives some gratuity to them. They are exceedingly gruff and harsh to the "unwashed mob," to the laboring man or mechanic, but to the well-dressed gentleman, who bears outward evidence that he has money in his pocket, these "pompous turkey-cocks" are exceedingly attentive, and almost annoying. The fact is, the mechanic or laboring man has about as much chance in society in England, as a feline animal has in that hot country we read about, without pedal extremities, wherewithal to defend herself.

"The Tunnel" of the Thames is an object of great attraction. It is one of the wonders of the metropolis. It is situated about two miles below London Bridge. It is a work of great skill and untiring energy, planned and completed by Sir Isambert Brunel. It is a hollow brick tube, divided into two roadways, each 15 feet high and 12 feet broad. It cost nearly $2,000,000, and is considered bad stock, as it does not pay one per cent. interest on the money invested. At each end of the tunnel there is a place of descent, or cylindrical shaft, of 100 steps, by which foot passengers pass, on paying a toll of a penny. The tunnel is well kept, and appears to be perfectly safe; no water drips through, no stains even are on the sides, but all appears to be as secure as an ordinary dwelling above ground. It is occupied by a large number of girls, who sell books and trinkets of all sorts. There is also here a small printing press in constant use. A band of music is usually stationed here, who enliven the scene, and lighten your pockets of your coppers, by handing round the hat.

London contains 760 churches; of these, 370 belong to the Established Church; 25 to the Roman Catholic; Independents, 130; Methodists, 120; Baptists, 100; Congregationalists, 38; Presbyterians, 18; Mormons, 13; Jews, 12; Unitarians, 7, and Lutherans, 6. There are others, but not numerous.

St. Paul's Cathedral is the largest and best known edifice in the city. It is built on the top of Ludgate Hill. Its architect, Sir Christopher Wren, considered himself peculiarly fortunate to have lived until this greatest of all his works was completed. It is 510 feet in length, and 250 in breadth. The church is crowned with an immense dome, surmounted by a lantern, ball and cross, the height of the cross from the pavement being 404 feet. The columns which support the immense dome, are of the Corinthian and composite orders, and are 222 feet high. This vast structure is built entirely of Portland stone, at a cost of about $4,000,000. In this cathedral are buried Sir Ralph Abercromby, Sir John Moore, Dr. Samuel Johnson, Howard, and Sir Joshua Reynolds, the great painter. Here, also, underneath the great dome, lie Lord Nelson and the Duke of Wellington.

After St. Paul's, is Westminster Abbey. This I have in a previous letter described to you. It is by far the finest ecclesiastical edifice in England, and one of the very best specimens of the pointed style. In this old and venerated Abbey, are crowned the kings and queens of Great Britain, and here many of them are buried, their earthly crowns being laid aside, and are now awaiting that "dread trump," at whose sound king and queen, prince and people, high and low, must all come, and in His awful presence bow the head and bend the knee.

There are many other fine churches in London. Among them are St. Bartholomew's, in Smithfield; St. Stephen's, in Walbrook; Bow Church; St. Bride's in Fleet Street, and St. Martin's-in-the-Fields, all fine specimens of their peculiar style.

For the Rev. Mr. Spurgeon, a Baptist clergyman, a huge church is now being built, which I should think would hold, when completed, 10,000 persons.

I regret that it will be impossible for me to write you much more about this great city. There are hundreds of interesting places and things here, to tell of which it would fill a volume. The parks of London are delightful places for recreation and fresh air. Hyde Park is the largest. It contains 400 acres, and lies between Uxbridge and Kensington roads. In it is an artificial lake, called the Serpentine. A small portion or strip of this park is railed off for equestrians, and is called "Rotten

Row." Here lords and ladies, on fine blooded steeds, are daily seen exercising themselves. Next is St. James's Park, 83 acres, and extends from Buckingham Palace to the Horse Guards. On the north side of London is Regent's Park, 403 acres. Round this Park is a delightful drive, nearly two miles in length. Here are the Botanical and Zoological Gardens, which are exceedingly interesting to the curious traveller, or the man of science. Here I saw a "laughing hyena." The keeper, in feeding him, would hold up to his cage a piece of meat, and tell him to laugh a little. The impatient animal would break out into the most unearthly screams, imitating in a remarkable degree the loud and wild laugh of a maniac.

The Queen is not here. She is on the Isle of Wight at Osborne; consequently I have not seen her. I shall go to Osborne expressly to see her Majesty, for whom I have a very high regard. Mr. Charles Dickens is also absent from town—out in the country at his residence, Strawberry Hill. I called on Dr. Samuel Warren, the author of the "Diary of a Physician," and "Ten Thousand a Year." He entertained me very handsomely, and asked a thousand questions about our country and our men of letters. He is an elegant gentleman, and exceedingly genial in his manners.

My friend and travelling companion, Dr. Smith, has returned from the land of "Brither Scots," and is hurrying me off to Paris. Napoleon is there with his Italian army, fresh from Magenta and Solferino. He proposes to make a grand *entrée* on the 12th, and like the great Pompey or Julius Cæsar, bring his "trophies into Rome." It will be a great day, a glorious day, for excitable, fête-loving Paris. Napoleon is a great man. He has whipped the Austrians and freed Italy, but he never can whip the English. They eat too much roast beef here, and drink too much ale, ever to be whipped. I am satisfied that England will never be conquered so long as she is true to herself. Her bold peasantry love their native land. Her lords and titled gentry are always foremost on the battle-field, and go where the danger is the greatest. She is arming now for the contest, and will meet her enemy, whoever he may be, foot to foot, and beard to beard.

By the way, the fighting men of London are patronized here by the highest dignitaries of state. I went with a friend to see the "Fancy," and saw the "ugly mug" of Tom Sayers. He is well "put up" from the ground, but a much smaller man than I expected to see. He says "that he can whip any man that walks shoe-leather." May be so, may be not. The "Boy," I am told, talks of coming over. He may at least worry him a little. One good blow from him, I think, would break Tom's shoulder or crack his "nut."

I went to the Royal Italian Opera last night, at the Covent Garden. The opera was "le Pardon de Ploermel," by Meyerbeer. The house is a magnificent establishment; audience very fashionable, and music delightful. London is a great city: great in its raggedness and its vice—great in its learning, its arts and sciences—but greater still in its Christianity and its noble charities.

Yours truly,
H. W. A.

LETTER NO. VIII.

Hotel du Louvre, Paris, *August* 13, 1859.

Editors Advocate:

I arrived in this great centre of fashion and elegance on the 7th instant, and have, by the assistance of a cab, a stallion and a courier, seen a good deal of what may be termed "real life in Paris." The Neapolitans say, "see Naples and die;" but I say, see Paris and never say die, but live as long as you possibly can, for certainly there are more inducements held out here to the living, than any other city in the world. From London to Paris is twelve hours. Fare £3 1s. 6d. All the way to Dover you pass through the counties of Surrey and Kent, the poorest in all England. Immense beds of chalk crop out in every direction. The principal production of the soil is hops, which command a high price, and are used in large quantities by the numerous breweries in the country. Dover is a queer-looking old place. Here are those celebrated Shakspeare cliffs, which the immortal bard has described so sublimely:

> "How fearful
> And dizzy 'tis to cast one's eyes so low!
> The crows and choughs that wing the midway air
> Show scarce so gross as beetles; halfway down
> Hangs one that gathers samphire—dreadful trade!
> Methinks he seemes no bigger than his head.
> The fishermen that walk upon the beach
> Appear like mice. I'll look no more,
> Lest my brain turn, and the deficient sight
> Topple down headlong."

I did not find these aforesaid cliffs of such immense height. Shakspeare has certainly taken a good deal of poetic license, for they look very much like "Ellis' Cliffs" near Natchez, or the Port Hudson bluffs—not an inch higher!

As to the "samphire man," I did not see him at all, at all. From Dover to Calais, the distance across the English Channel is short—only twenty miles. You can see the French coast very plainly, the nearest point being seventeen miles. The day I crossed was very calm, but still I became very sea-sick. The waves are short, and in seamen's phrase, "choppy." This causes the vessel to rock in a most wretched manner, and strange to say, makes one more sea-sick than crossing the ocean. On my arrival at Calais, a very polite Frenchman (a commissionaire) came forward, took charge of my baggage and passport—had all put through in short order, and left me to eat my dinner in peace.

Here we found the most delicious fruit; peaches, figs and grapes, and the most delightful claret. From Calais to Paris is quite a long distance, 235 miles. We passed through St. Omer, celebrated for its ancient college of the Jesuits, now dwindled almost to insignificance—thence through Lille, a large city, particularly remarkable for its manufactures of thread, gloves and linen. This place has been the scene of many bloody battles in the early history of France; for being near the frontier, it was often attacked by the enemy. The entire city is surrounded by immense fortifications, consisting of walls and ditches, scarps and counterscarps, and every thing else that the genius of the great Vauban could invent.

Passing through Douay and Valenciennes, both very renowned cities, the one for books and the other for fine laces, we arrived in Paris, and put up at the Hotel du Louvre, an immense concern, gotten up in a most magnificent style, and partly on the American plan. It is the head-quarters for Americans, and at present is crowded with "those occidentals." There are to-day, I am informed, 1,500 persons at the Hotel. The English custom is pretty well carried out, with the exception of a table d'hôte. You take your room and pay for it. If you eat at the Hotel, you are charged as at a restaurant. The restaurant is the great eating place of Paris. Everybody seems to patronize the café for breakfast, and the restaurant for dinner. The celebrated Trois Frères is assuredly a very elegant establishment, and they give you there a magnificent dinner and a good bottle of wine, but it is not superior to Victor's in New Orleans. Victor will give you just as good a bottle of wine as you can get in Paris, and I don't know but a little better, for we all know that a sea voyage improves claret, while Burgundy is the only wine that does not bear transportation. Wines are generally better here, and much cheaper than with us.

In public buildings, statuary and painting, in fountains and flowers, in music and dancing, and pirouetting, in all these Paris excels the world. The Palace of the Luxembourg is the most gorgeous, I presume, ever built by the ingenuity of man. I have seen the royal chambers in Windsor Castle, and Buckingham, the most splendid in England, but they will not begin to compare with the salle du trone of the Luxembourg. This is a vast room whose walls are covered with rare paintings, while the ceiling is almost an entire fresco. In this hall are the statues of the great Napoleon and Julius Cæsar. So many are the paintings and so dazzling is this imperial hall, that the visitor becomes bewildered, and is almost pained with the excess of splendor. The Hotel des Invalides is full of interest. It is one of the largest edifices in Paris, and contains in its capacious apartments the old soldiers of the empire, who have become wounded in battle or infirm by age. In the front portion of this immense edifice, on the left hand as you enter, lie the remains of the great Napoleon, surrounded by the flags that he took in his numerous battles. Here the lights are always kept burning, and the crowd is so great to see the coffin of this wonderful man, that many have to wait for hours before they can even get near the railing which surrounds the sacred relics. Such is imperishable glory. Napoleon is now almost worshipped as a god; and if it were possible for him to rise from the dead and walk the streets of Paris, all France would go completely crazy with enthusiasm.

The churches here are very fine, and full of rare paintings by the old masters. Notre Dame is perhaps the most remarkable. In it the Te Deums are chanted on grand state occasions. Here the Emperor and Empress frequently go to Mass, and from the tower of this old church was thrown one of the Archbishops of France, by a certain Hunchback, according to our friend Victor Hugo.

The Madeleine is the most chaste and elegant building in Paris. It is built after the style of the Parthenon in Athens, and is surrounded by immense Corinthian pillars. Here also are many fine paintings.

The Pantheon is another magnificent church. This contains the apotheosis of Napoleon. In the immense dome is a splendid fresco painting. It is "La Mort Patrie La Justice, Gloire." In the last is *Napoleon embracing glory*. This painting attracts thousands to see it, and you daily meet old and young, prince and peasant, men and women, with upturned faces gazing in mute admiration and astonishment at this great triumph of the "divine art."

I must close this letter. To-day I went to Père la Chaise, the great Cemetery of Paris. In wandering through it I came to the graves of Heloise and Abelard. These are surrounded with a plain iron railing. I noticed that the tombs were covered with many wreaths and flowers, brought by all classes as offerings to the constancy of love. My courier took me to the grave of Massena. A splendid monument rises to his memory, but shame to tell it, by the side of Massena lie the mortal remains of Marshal Ney, the bravest of the brave, without even a head-stone to mark the spot. Père la Chaise is a democratic burial-ground. Prince and peasant, rich and poor, high and low, are all here together in close proximity, each awaiting the final trump of the archangel.

> "The glories of our birth and state
> Are shadows, not substantial things.
> There is no armor against fate—
> Death lays his icy hand on kings;
> Sceptre and crown must tumble down,
> And in the dust be equal made
> With the poor crooked scythe and spade."

Good-bye. I shall write you again from this city, and give you a bird's-eye view of some of the "mysteries of Paris."

Yours, truly,
H. W. A.

LETTER NO. IX.

Hotel de la Meslopole, Geneva, Switzerland,
August 20, 1859.

Editors Advocate:

From Paris to this city is twelve hours by rail. The weather being exceedingly warm, we have suffered very much. For many miles after leaving Paris, I find the country rather tame and exceedingly poor, particularly through the departments of Seine and Marne, and the Yonne. But few grapes are grown in this part of France. On entering the Cote d'Or, however, I found the hills clad with vines, and all nature giving evidences of a rich and genial soil. This is the heart of Burgundy, and here is Dijon, an old town, its former capital. The "House of Burgundy" has played a very important part in the history of the world, for Mary and Margaret have both left their marks in the "Book of Time," while the "Dukes" were important personages, even in the presence of royalty itself. Besides, a certain dark-colored beverage, called Burgundy wine, has for centuries had a very perceptible influence upon the heads and hearts, the nerves and brains, the minds and bodies of half the crowned heads of Europe. This old town is rich in the history of the middle ages. It possesses a museum, a picture gallery, and a cabinet of Natural History. The place looks exceedingly quiet. It has a Place d'Armes or public square, in the shape of a horseshoe, which is in front of the ancient palaçe of the dukes of Burgundy. Those delicious wines, Chambertin and Romance, are still made here in this immediate neighborhood. They are just as good now as they were in the days of the great Napoleon, who preferred them to all others. These rich Burgundy wines do not bear transportation like the Rhine wines, or those of the south of France, consequently no man who has not visited France, can even imagine what a real good bottle of Burgundy is. There is a richness and a delicious bouquet about this wine which no other possesses. It comes as near the nectar of the gods as any thing earthly can, for I believe in my soul that St. Anthony himself, who resisted all other temptations, could not resist a bottle—aye, a couple of bottles of pure, unadulterated, untravelled Chambertin!

Leaving Dijon, the face of the country becomes hilly and then mountainous, for we soon strike the Department of Jura, the Franche-Comté of the old *régime*. Here the mountains begin to crop out on all sides, for you are soon in the very heart of that long chain of "Jura's rugged heights," which separates France from Switzerland. The French are close cultivators, but are far behind the English in the art of husbandry. They are generally small landholders, and consequently there are no fine castles or elegant lordly mansions in the country. You see neat cottages and pretty chateaus, surrounded with smiling vineyards and gaily dressed "nut-brown" maids, all of which is very agreeable and quite romantic.

I stopped at a vineyard in Burgundy, and inquired what price they paid their laborers. I was informed that the men were paid two francs per day during the vintage season, and the women one franc, board and lodging included; and strange to tell, each laborer drank eight bottles of wine per day! This seems almost incredible, but I have it from the very best authority. Every laboring peasant will drink two bottles of wine for his breakfast, two for his dinner, one for his supper, and the rest between meals, for your honest Frenchman despises water! He never takes it.

Well, let us return to Geneva, for here we are in sight of Mont Blanc, that looms up like a huge spectre in the distance. This is an old, and rather queer-looking city, delightfully situated on the lake Geneva, and at the head of the Rhone. Here the Rhone issues from the lake, in a few hundred yards receives the Arve, (a turgid stream coming down from the glaciers,) and passing Lyons, empties itself into the Mediterranean Sea. The meet-

ing of the Arve and the Rhone is very similar to
that of the Missouri and Mississippi—only on a
much smaller scale, for neither of these celebrated
streams is larger than the Amite. It was here, in
Geneva, that Jean Jacques Rousseau, son of a
watchmaker, was born. 'Twas here that his first
book, the Emile, was publicly burnt by the common hangman, and strange to say, it was here that
Voltaire assisted in this persecution. The house
where Jean Jacques (as he is called) was born, is
shown to the curious traveller. On a beautiful
island where the Rhone issues from the lake, is a
bronze statue placed on granite, of this remarkable
man.

It was here also that John Calvin, the great
Reformer, lived. He came to Geneva as an itinerant preacher flying from Rome, and in a few years
became the Dictator of the Republic. From the
Cathedral St. Pierre he thundered forth his severe
denunciations against the corruptions of the times.
Here he entertained John Knox when driven out
of Scotland, and here it was that he ordered Servetus to be led to the stake for entertaining religious
opinions not exactly orthodox. This is one of the
darkest spots on Calvin's character, for he was a
great and good man, and his memory here is much
revered. He has left his mark behind him. A
very large and respectable community, both in the
old and new world, are his followers. His name
will live as long as the Bible, for he was one of its
greatest expounders. In the Cemetery of the Plain

Palais, on the banks of the Rhone, lie the mortal remains of John Calvin. No monumental marble marks his grave, but simply a plain rough granite stone, on which is cut J. C.

Geneva is a small city, only numbering about 40,000 inhabitants—still she, by her sons, has had a wonderful influence in the affairs of this world. In Theology, there was Calvin; in Literature, Rousseau and Voltaire; in Politics, Neckar and Dumont; in Science, De Saussure, and Huber, and De Luc. Among the living great men are De La Rive, the Chemist; Mannoir, the Oculist, and Merle d'Aubigné, the Historian.

Geneva is improving very rapidly. It has become a great place for fine classic schools, principally supported by English and Americans. Here is the place to learn the modern languages. The present occupation of the great majority of its laboring population, is the manufacture of watches, jewelry, and musical instruments. The jewellers' shops here are very fine—you can buy a good gold watch for $40, while diamonds and other precious stones sell for about one-half of what we have to pay in New Orleans. The water of lake Geneva is a deep indigo blue, while the high mountains which surround it give it the most romantic and picturesque appearance.

I leave to-morrow for Mont Blanc and the Vale of Chamouni in Savoy, and shall write you again from the region of eternal snow. Adieu.

Yours, truly,

H. W. A.

LETTER NO. X.

Geneva, Switzerland, *August* 24, 1859.

Rev. Z. Butler, D. D., *Port Gibson, Miss.:*

My Dear Sir—Inclosed I send you a sprig of fern, which I pulled from a tree that grows over the grave of John Calvin. Immediately upon my arrival here I procured a courier, and hastened off in search—first, of Calvin's house; second, his church; and third, his grave. They all are shown. His house in which he lived has been so much changed and remodelled, that scarcely a vestige of the old mansion remains. His church, the venerable St. Pierre, is still standing in its awful grandeur, and is visited by thousands of strangers, from every land. On entering it, I found a plain Gothic structure, of extreme simplicity. It is one of the finest uncorrupted specimens of Gothic architecture of the eleventh century, now in existence. I am just from Paris, where there are many churches, whose walls are covered with fine paintings, and whose ceilings are brilliant with frescoes. How different is this venerable old Protestant cathedral. Not one painting hangs on its aged walls—no frescoes adorn its ceilings. In this church are but two monuments. One to the great Huguenot, Comte Henri de Rohan, and Agrippa d'Aubigny, friend of Henry IV., and the grandfather of the celebrated Madame de Maintenon. In the centre of the paved floor lie buried the remains of Cardinal Broglie, who presided at the trial of John Huss, and who stood by the stake and saw the man of God receive the martyr's crown. With the consent of the sexton, I walked up into the pulpit. While seated in the chair of Calvin, I thought of the stirring times of this great reformer. It was from this very spot that he denounced the prevailing immorality of Geneva, with such eloquence and force, that profligacy was obliged to hide its head. The pulpit of St. Pierre became at once his tribune and his judgment-seat, and his hearers, adopting a vigorous and puritanical austerity of manners, punished with severity every transgression of Calvin's code of morals.

Geneva still holds on to her Protestant faith, although the influence of France and French manners and customs is very strong, and the outside pressure very great. For many years one of the austere laws of Calvin prohibited theatres, and it has only been very recently that a "salle de spectacle" has been built. Three-fourths of Geneva are Protestants—the rest being Jews and Romanists.

From the cathedral I went to the Cemetery of

Plain Palais, on the banks of the Rhone, and there was shown the grave of John Calvin. On his death he requested that no monument of any kind should be erected over his grave, and now nothing but a plain, rough, granite head-stone marks the place where he was buried. On the stone is this simple and short inscription—" J. C." In 1536 Calvin passed through Geneva as a fugitive from Italy to Basle. Here he was invited to stop by Farel. He did so, and soon the itinerant preacher became the dictator of the republic. For twenty-three years he ruled with uninterrupted power. This wonderful man died quite young, being only fifty-five, but he has left his mark. In the then small town of Geneva he sowed the seeds of a faith, that has brought forth abundant fruit in Scotland, in England, in France, in Germany, and Switzerland. This same faith was transported by the Pilgrim fathers to our own country, and this same faith had much to do with a certain paper called "The Declaration of Independence."

"'Tis bound by a thousand bands to my heart."

It was my father's and mother's faith—it shall always be mine. Geneva is a beautiful place, with a population of about 40,000 inhabitants. It is situated most beautifully on the lake, and at the foot of the Alps. Mont Blanc is seen in the distance like a huge spectre, covered with eternal snows.

The English and Americans seem to have selected this place to educate their children, and by their patronage have built up fine schools. The principal occupation of the inhabitants is watch-making, and the manufacture of jewelry and musical instruments. A good many books are also published here, while this is the depot for the finest wine district of Switzerland. A good bottle of wine can be had here for thirty-seven and a half cents, and a fine gold watch for forty dollars.

Switzerland is crowded with Americans. Like the locusts of Egypt, "they are infesting the land." They climb every noted rock, and cut their names in *big letters*. The altar of Notre Dame in Paris is pencilled all over with names of Americans, while the pulpit of John Calvin bears strong testimony to the cutting qualities of a Yankee's pocket-knife.

While in London, I went to the Surrey Gardens, on Sunday, to hear the celebrated Rev. Mr. Spurgeon. He had an immense audience, some six or eight thousand; choice seats, that is, front or near seats, being sold at twenty-five cents each. After the entire audience had been quietly seated, the reverend gentleman made his appearance, walked hurriedly to the pulpit, (placed nearly in the centre of the vast hall,) and commenced immediately divine service, by reading the hymn, "Come thou fount of every blessing." He then gave out the hymn by verse or stanza. The whole audience joined in singing. After singing was prayer, and then he read a chapter from the Bible, and explained it as he read. Then he gave out the hymn, "Rock of

Ages." His reading of this hymn was somewhat theatrical, but its effect was great. After singing all but the last verse, he stopped, and requested his hearers to sing the last in a slow and solemn manner. I looked around, and I do believe that every person in that vast assemblage joined in singing. The effect was astonishing, for when the hymn was ended, there was scarcely a dry eye in the congregation. He took his text from Matthew xi. 29—read it over twice—closed the book, and without note or comment, or memorandum, kept his congregation spell-bound for two hours. He does not rant or tear a passion into tatters, but is earnest and persuasive. His voice is very similar to that of the Rev. Daniel Baker, in his palmiest days. Mr. Spurgeon is certainly a very great man. He is only 23 years old, and is a great prodigy as an orator. His personal appearance is very prepossessing, while his unpretending address secures the love and admiration of all who approach him. His congregation are now building for him an immense tabernacle, that will hold twenty thousand persons. What a great pity it is that so promising a man, so truly eloquent a divine, should leave the path the Saviour trod, and enter into the dirty pool of abolitionism. This has injured his influence very much, especially with Americans, who seem to think that he had better confine his sympathies and his charities to the overworked and emaciated white slaves of Manchester and Glasgow.

In Liverpool and Belfast, particularly in Belfast, there is preaching in the open air, in the streets, and on the commons, at all times of the day. You are aware that there is a deadly feud between the Orangemen and the Romanists of Ireland; every year, at the celebration of the battle of the Boyne, Belfast was in a general row, and many bloody heads and broken bones was the consequence. I was told that the revival in the north of Ireland has quieted down the turbulent spirits, and those who were the greatest rowdies have become good, peaceable citizens.

My dear sir, I see that I have written you a long letter, much longer than I intended. I know, however, that you will appreciate it, for it comes from one who has always loved you.

I leave to-morrow morning for Mont Blanc and the vale of Chamouni, thence to Basle down the Rhine to Cologne. I may write you again from the "eternal city," for I shall be in Rome in ten days from to-day.

Yours, sincerely,
H. W. A.

LETTER NO. XI.

Vale of Chamouni, *Aug.* 22, 1859.

"Mont Blanc is the monarch of mountains,
 They crowned him long ago,
On a throne of rocks, in a robe of clouds,
 With a diadem of snow."

Editors Advocate:

From Geneva, I took *diligence*, and in ten hours arrived at this place, passing through much beautiful Swiss scenery. A few miles from Geneva we passed the limits of Switzerland, and had to have our passports *visaed* by a Savoyard armed with a big moustache and a long sword. Just as soon as we got fairly into the Alps, we met with the most disgusting objects of goitre, exposed, as beggars, on the roadside. Women and children seem to be the most afflicted with this terrible disease.

After a long drive and a longer walk over hill and mountain, we at last arrived in this beautiful valley, which is indeed almost an Elysium. To the lover of nature and nature's boldest and wildest works, here is the place to linger. Mont Blanc, covered with eternal snow, lifts his proud and haughty head far above all other terrene objects, while the Glaciers, those wonderful freaks of nature, are seen here in all their grandeur and glory. It is truly a delightful feeling on this the 22d day of August, while the sun is at its meridian, to be standing on a sea of ice. I took a guide and a mule, and ascended the Alps, until I came to the great "Mer de Glace," so much spoken of by naturalists. With the assistance of my guide, I crossed this sea of ice with great difficulty. It is about a mile wide and fifty miles long, averaging, as far as can be ascertained, two hundred feet deep. During the hot weather of summer, there is a continual thawing of the ice going on, and a gradual, daily movement of the whole mass. From the foot of this Glacier flows the river Arveyron, formed by the melting of the ice. It rushes down the mountain at railroad speed : so terrible is its descent, that none escape who are so unfortunate as to fall therein. The ice of the "Mer de Glace" is pure white, tinged with blue, and is rent into many deep and perpendicular crevices, into which the water flows with the sound of distant thunder. In the upper portion of this sea of ice, is what is called the "Jardin." It is a large rock about seven acres in extent, covered over with mosses and lichens, and Alpine flowers, and entirely surrounded with ice. The effect is most beautiful indeed. Like a green oasis in the desert, it stands in the midst of desolation, inviting the traveller to come and rest his weary limbs. If I only possessed Aladdin's lamp, and could summon to my assistance some of his strong-armed genii, I would immediately transport this "Mer de Glace," with its beautiful "Jardin," to Baton Rouge. Although it might interfere somewhat with the business of your respected fellow-townsman, Mr. Mann, still, I think it would have a tendency to *keep your politicians cool* for several years to come, and then there would have to be no more *extravagant* appropriations for the State House grounds, for the Alpine flowers would supply the place of *those magnolias*. One great curiosity about the Glaciers is this: they create in melting, so to speak, an artificial atmosphere, and exist near the foot of the mountains, some even at the very base. Wheat fields extend up to the very ice, and cattle graze up to the Glaciers, and often walk over them. Every year some village or other is swept away by an avalanche.

The Savoyards are a quiet, ignorant, and degraded people. They furnish us with our organ-grinders. The women here perform much of the manual labor—they plough, cut wheat, mow hay and pack immense loads on their heads, for I have not seen a cart or wagon as yet in Savoy.

Tuesday morning.—You see that I am still travelling. From Chamouni I went to Martigny, a distance of twenty-five miles, on a mule, over the highest and most picturesque portion of the Alps. The road or path in many places is dug around high cliffs, and through immense mountains. The head swims in passing these places, while even the mules seem to know the danger, and hug the sides of the mountain as close as possible. From Chamouni to Martigny the route is only performed by mules, or on foot. In this neighborhood is made the delightful Gruyères cheese, which is so much sought after in our country. The cheese-makers take their cows to the mountains, and in their chalets (that is, cottages) far off from human habitations, they make the cheese during summer, and in the fall bring it down and keep it till spring, when it is ready for sale. This cheese is very delicious here. We do not get the real Gruyères in the United States. It will not bear exportation. If I can find room in my *trunk* on my return home, I will take you a piece about the size of a grindstone, (for they look more like grindstones than any thing else.)

I leave Martigny this morning for the Castle of Chillon and Lausanne, thence back to Geneva. Adieu. I shall write you again from the banks of the Rhine.

Yours, very truly,
H. W. A.

LETTER NO. XII.

Berne, Capital of Switzerland,
Aug. 25, 1859.

Editors Advocate:

I wrote you last from Martigny. From this place, I took rail for the Lake of Geneva, going down the Rhone to its mouth at Bovart. The Rhone, like the Mississippi, is yearly making land far out into the Lake; already within the memory of the living, an immense marsh has been formed, which resembles very much the delta of our great river. The fishermen have a very curious way of catching fish in the Rhone. They wade into the water, at night, with a knife and a water-tight lamp. They place the lamp under water, and the trout will soon follow it. As the fish come up to the surface of the water, the fisherman kills them with his knife. This is no fish story, but a veritable fact.

Arm yourselves, my dear sirs, with a good butcher knife and a lantern, go to the Amite or Lake Cocodrie, and you will come back perfectly *scaly* with fish. Tell our friend W. S. Pike, to throw his patent poles, his bobs and sinkers, his worms and flies, all to the dogs or the d—l, and act as a sensible man should, and catch fish by the light of the moon in a sensible way.

From Bovart I took steamer, and in an hour was at Vevay. This is a remarkable place for wines and cheese, also for being near the celebrated Castle of Chillon, about which Lord Byron has written one of his most beautiful poems. The Castle still stands, and is kept in good repair.

> " Lake Leman lies by Chillon's walls,
> A thousand feet in depth below,
> Its massy waters meet and flow,
> A double dungeon wall and wave
> Have made—and like a living grave."

This castle was built by one of the kings of Savoy, in 1238, and was long used as a state prison, where, among other victims, many of the early reformers were chained to the seven huge columns. The rings are still fast in these columns, and the damp pavement beneath the deep waters is worn away by the constant passing of the prisoners. It was in this deep cell that Byron's ideal prisoner, Bonnivard, was chained. In his own mournful but beautiful language he says:

> " And then there was a little isle
> Which to my very face did smile,
> The only one in view;
> A small green isle, it seemed no more,
> Scarce broader than my dungeon floor:

> But in it there were three tall trees,
> And o'er it blew the mountain breeze,
> And by it there were waters flowing,
> And on it there were young flowers growing
>   Of gentle breath and hue."

The description is perfect, for just opposite the castle, and near the mouth of the Rhone, there is this pretty little isle, no larger than "a dungeon floor," with only three trees on it, and covered with flowers. It is much resorted to by tourists. On one of the columns of the castle dungeon, Byron has carved his name; Dickens has carved his, and John Smith, Bottle Green Jones, etc., have carved theirs. The Castle of Chillon is now used by the Swiss as a magazine for military stores. The Hotel Byron stands close by, and is crowded with visitors during the summer.

Around Vevay the country is most charming. Every foot of land is planted in vines—for miles and miles you see nothing but one solid vineyard, extending from the lake upwards to the top of the mountains. Here the very best champagne is sold at four francs a bottle, *vin ordinaire* at half a franc a bottle. From Vevay I went to Lausanne—stopped at the Hotel Gibbon. This is quite a large town, capital of the Canton Pays de Vaud, and is remarkable for having been the residence of the great historian. Here it was in this hotel that Gibbon penned that history of the Decline and Fall of the Roman Empire, which has made his name immortal. After finishing his great work he wrote these lines :

"It was on the day, or rather the night of the 27th of June, 1787, between the hours of eleven and twelve, that I wrote the last line of the last page in a summer-house in my garden. After laying down my pen, I took several turns in a berceau or covered walk of acacias, which commands a prospect of the country, the lake, and the mountains. The air was temperate, the sky was serene, the silver orb of the moon was reflected from the waves, and all nature was silent."

The air is still temperate, and the sky is still serene, but Gibbon is gone to his long home—his house has decayed, and but few of the acacias are left to mark the spot where he spent the happiest days of his life. Time will conquer all at last. The grandeur and glory of to-day lies humbled in the dust on to-morrow, while youth and beauty are the constant food for worms.

Of all that I have seen of earth, Mont Blanc alone defies Old Time. Seated on his throne of granite, he shakes his snowy locks at all around him, and laughs at the petty wars of man. He witnessed the crossing of the Alps by those great warriors Hannibal and Napoleon. He saw the fatal shaft as it entered the heart of the tyrant Gessler, and he now beholds a proud little republic, free, happy, and united.

From Lausanne I went up the lake, back to Geneva, thence by rail to Lake Neuchatel, up this lake to the town of Neuchatel. This is an important place in Switzerland, and has sent forth into the world many great men; among them Prof. Agassiz, of Cambridge College, Mass. Most of the watches sold in Geneva are manufactured at this place. Here are made the celebrated Neuchatel cheese and Swiss wine, very much used. Lake Neuchatel is very picturesque, and seems to be encircled with one immense vineyard. It lies between the Jura and the Alps, and empties its beautiful blue waters into Lake Bienne, through the river Thiele. Through this I passed—thence through Lake Bienne—thence by rail again to Berne. Here I called on our Minister, Mr. Fay, was very kindly treated, and had my passport visaed *again*. Berne is a very pretty place, romantically located on the high banks of the Aar. It has two fine old cathedrals and a Federal Palace. The palace is a beautiful building, just finished after the Moorish style of architecture. On entering it, the officer, learning that I was from America, gave me every attention, and conducted me through every apartment. It is neat and elegant, without any pretension of show or royal grandeur.

The Swiss are very kind to Americans, and express the warmest regard for our country. They still possess the same love of liberty that their fathers possessed, and carry the right of suffrage farther than we do, allowing every male over 18 years of age to vote.

In Berne I find clean streets, with numerous fountains, all representing *bears*. The bear is the national emblem—Bruin is even painted in fresco in the cathedrals.

The clock-tower is a great curiosity. At 12 (noon) a cock crows, and a small army of bears, mounted on horseback, march round, while a bearded figure in the centre marks the hours by opening and shutting his mouth.

I leave this evening for Zurich, and may take a hand in that celebrated Congress that is now there assembled. Adieu.

Yours truly,
H. W. A.

LETTER NO. XIII.

Lucerne, Switzerland, *August* 27, 1859.

Editors Advocate:

I wrote you last from Berne, I believe. From this place I took rail for Thun, a beautiful place on a lake of the same name: there I took steamer across Lake Thun to Interlaken, the most delightful watering place in Switzerland. It is, as its name imports, between two lakes—Lakes Thun and Brientz, and is frequented by all nations. The English, however, seem to have the predominance here. Lord Snob and Lady Upstart can be seen every evening riding out in fine carriages with liveried servants. The empress dowager of Russia is now here, where she spends the summer. She rents an entire hotel, the Belvidere, and lives in great style. From Interlaken I crossed Lake Brientz to the town of Brientz—thence on muleback across the Alps to Lake Lungern—thence down the lake to Aipnach on the Lake Lucerne—

thence across Lake Lucerne to the town of the same name. The town of Lucerne is a very pleasant place as a summer resort, having one of the very best hotels in Europe, the Switzer-Hof. Its population is about 10,000—all Catholics with a very few exceptions. Here the Pope's Nuncio resides. Situated between the giant mountains Pilatus and Regi and in sight of the snow-capped Alps, its scenery is considered the very finest in the world. The town possesses several curiosities which ought to be mentioned. First, the monument to the Swiss Guards who fell in 1792, at Paris, in defending the royal family of France. The design is by Thorwalsden, and executed by Ahorn. It represents a lion of colossal size wounded to death, with a spear sticking in his side, yet endeavoring in his last gasp to protect from injury a shield bearing the *fleur-de-lis* of the Bourbons, which he holds in his paws. The figure is hewn out of the living sandstone rock, (on the side of a high cliff,) is 28 feet long and 18 feet high, and whether as a tribute to fallen valor or as a work of art, it merits the highest praise. It is the most appropriate monument in Europe. The next thing of importance in Lucerne is the style of building or rather adorning their bridges—one of them is adorned with 77 fine paintings hung up in such a manner " that he who runs may read." The paintings are by Holbein, to represent the " Dance of Death." Here death is seen in 77 different shapes—and is intended as a warning to the living that we all must die—that "in the midst of life we are in death."

Lucerne is quite a manufacturing place. I saw several wagon-loads of American cotton passing through the streets from the railway to the various factories. On yesterday morning, I took a delightful trip up the lake Lucerne, which I found to be the most beautiful of all the lakes of Switzerland that I have thus far seen. From the town of Lucerne to the Bay of Uri, the lake seems a living panorama of gardens and vineyards—of green pastures and bright cottages. After passing the obelisk of Wytenstein, the Bay of Uri with all its stupendous grandeur bursts into view. It is upon this, that the superiority of the Lake of Lucerne to all other lakes depends. Vast mountains rising on every side and crowned with eternal snows—the soft spots of verdant pastures scattered at their feet—the placid lake, unbroken by islands and almost undisturbed by any signs of living men, make an impression which cannot be described. The town of Fluelen is situated on the Bay of Uri at the head of Lake Lucerne. Here is the place where William Tell shot the apple from his son's head—and on the very spot where he stood is a fountain, with the statue of Tell. On the spot where his son stood, or rather where he was tied to a tree, is another fountain, with the statue of Gessler. The distance is exactly 130 yards, for I stepped it myself, a pretty good shot for a bow and arrow. Near this place Tell was born, and only two miles below is his chapel, where he leaped from the boat during the storm, his chains having been taken off. The tyrant Gessler landed soon after and hastened home, but was intercepted by Tell and shot with his unerring arrow. This chapel is in a very romantic spot. At the foot of it is a perpendicular mountain, while the lake descends abruptly to the depth of 800 feet. In the chapel are fresco paintings as large as life of Tell's history, also of the assembling of the three patriots of Switzerland at the spring of Grutli just opposite, who first conceived the bold idea of freeing Switzerland. These are sacred spots to every Switzer, and like devout Mussulmans to Mecca, they make pilgrimages to see these sacred places. Once every year, on the first Friday after the Ascension, mass is said and a sermon is preached in Tell's chapel; the inhabitants on the lake repair hither in boats and form an aquatic procession, the like of which can only be seen in Switzerland.

"Sweet Lake of Lucerne, I now bid adieu
  To your mountains of green and your waters of blue;
  At the chapel of Tell, at Grutli's bold spring,
  Thy maidens shall yearly assemble and sing
  The praises of those who fell in the cause
  Of Switzerland's freedom, religion, and laws."

I leave to-day for Zurich, thence to Basle and Baden-Baden. Adieu.

Yours very truly,

H. W. A.

LETTER NO. XIV.

Zurich, Switzerland, Hotel Baur, 1859.

Editors Advocate:

I arrived here last evening late at night, direct from Berne. Owing to the immense ranges of high mountains all through this country, I had to go by rail nearly to Basle, and then up to Zurich. I had heard so much of this place, of its wealth and intelligence, its classic renown and its lovely scenery, that I determined to see it before leaving Switzerland. And then again, many years ago, when I was a boy, I had heard a beautiful girl in Mississippi sing, in a truly captivating and languishing style, that song which I then thought was almost angelic music. I mean "On the banks of Zurich's sweet waters." I have not heard that "boarding-school" melody for many a long year, but whenever I think of it, raven locks, and pearly teeth, and sweet pouting lips and languishing eyes, come right up before me in all their loveliness, and cause even at this day a slight palpitation of the heart.

While upon the subject of songs, I must tell you of the "Ranz de vaches." I heard it last night for the second time since I have been in Switzerland. I had just retired to bed, and although very much fatigued, after hearing this wild mountain song I could not sleep for hours. The thoughts of home, and joyous faces, and happy friends came gushing up before me, and seemed to oppress my very soul. I give you from a good Swiss authority, the following description of this great national melody, which will be read with much interest by your many readers:

"It is not uncommon to fine the Ranz de vaches spoken of by persons unacquainted with Switzerland and the Alps, as a single air, whereas they are a class of melodies prevailing among and peculiar to the Alpine valleys. Almost every valley has an air of its own, but the original air is said to be that of Appenzell. Their effect in producing home-sickness in the heart of the Swiss mountaineer, when heard in a distant land, and the prohibition of this music in the Swiss regiments in the service of France, on account of the number of desertions occasioned by it, are stories often repeated and founded on fact. These national songs are particularly wild in their character, yet full of melody; the choruses consist of a few remarkable shrill notes, uttered by a peculiar falsetto intonation in the throat. They originate in the practice of the shepherds on the Alps, of communicating with one another at the distance of a mile or more, by pitching the voice high. The name Ranz de vaches (German, Kuhreihen) literally means *cow-rows*, and is obviously derived from the order in which the cows march home at milking time, in obedience to the shepherd's call, communicating by the voice or through the Alp horn, a simple tube of wood wound round with bark, five or six feet long, admitting of but slight modulation, yet very melodious when caught up and prolonged by the mountain echoes. In some of the remoter pastoral districts of Switzerland, from which the ancient simplicity of manners is not altogether banished, the Alp horn supplies on the higher pastures where no church is near, the place of the vesper bell. The cow herd, posted on the highest peak, as soon as the sun has set, pours forth the first four or five notes of the Psalm, 'Praise God the Lord.' The same notes are repeated from distant Alps, and all within hearing, uncovering their heads and bending their knees, repeat their evening orison; after which the cattle are penned in their stalls, and the shepherds betake themselves to rest."

This description is from high authority, and is true to the letter, but on last night the "Ranz de vaches" was most shamefully desecrated. It was sang with great effect in the streets of Zurich by a band of rollicking youth, who seemed to be on a general "burst." The great Addison was much surprised to find that the little boys in Paris spoke French! But I confess that I was not at all astonished to see the *big boys* of Zurich on "a bend-er," for the wine here is very good, and the lager is really delicious.

Zurich, the most important manufacturing town in Switzerland, and the capital of a canton, has a population of 17,000 inhabitants, nearly all Protestants. It is situated on the north end of Lake Zurich, and on the banks of the Limmatt River, just where it issues out of the lake. The banks of the lake and the river, and all the neighboring hills, are thickly dotted over with beautiful houses, built generally in the romantic Swiss style. There are no very fine public buildings here. The cathedral, surmounted by two steeples, is venerable for its age, having been built in the 10th century, and is worthy of respect from having been the scene of Zwingli's bold preachings of Reformation. It is a massive Romanesque edifice, very plain within and without. The house in which the great Reformer himself lived, is still standing in the Grosse stadt, and is an object of general attraction. The next church of much interest is St. Peter's. It stands on the left bank of the Limmatt, and had for its pastor for 23 years the celebrated Lavater, the author of the renowned work on physiognomy. This divine met with a melancholy fate. On the capture of the town by the French army, he was shot within a few steps of his own door, by a French soldier, whom he had treated with great kindness and liberality. A high reward was offered by Massena, the French general, for the discovery of the murderer, but the good Lavater refused to inform against him. Lavater died on the 2d January, 1801. His grave is marked by a simple stone in the churchyard of St. Anne.

In the Town Library are many volumes and manuscripts of rare merit. Among them I saw three Latin letters of Lady Jane Grey to Bullinger, in a beautiful, clear, and regular hand; also Zwingli's Greek Bible, with marginal notes by himself. Zurich has its university, which is flourishing very well, but it is as a manufacturing town that this place is chiefly remarkable. Silks and cottons are here spun and woven into all sorts of tissues, and are the objects of extensive commerce with Italy and Germany. There are also very extensive iron foundries and machine-shops here, where all the lake steamers are made, many being hauled across the mountains on wagons, and then put together at their place of destination. Not only are there many large manufacturing establishments in Zurich, but I noticed all along the lake, the brilliant colors of the calicoes exposed to the sun, by acres and acres. Lake Zurich is one of the most charming sheets of water of mountainous, romantic Switzerland. It is 23 miles long, averaging 1 mile wide, and is especially remarkable for the peculiar softness of its scenery. Here is none of the wild and savage grandeur of Lake Lucerne, nor is there the oppressive stillness of the barren heaths of Loch Lomond, but the song of the vine-dresser and the busy hum of a thriving and industrious population are heard in every direction. The slopes of the hills surrounding this beautiful lake may be called one immense vineyard. Here the vine grows to great perfection, and yields a very delicious wine. The Canton of Zurich may be said to be more hilly than mountainous. The grasses, wheat, rye, barley, oats, and corn grow here very well, and are produced in large quantities, for the Swiss farmers are proverbial for their great success in the application of fertilizers.

The German language is spoken here; at Geneva they speak French, and in St. Gall and the Grisons Italian, or a corrupt Latin called Romanish. Notwithstanding these peculiarities or differences of language, the Swiss have lived so long in a state of confederation, that they have acquired a decided national character, and may now be considered as forming a single people. The surroundings of the town of Zurich are really most delightful. In the new Botanical Garden there is an elevated mound called the Cat's Bastion. Nothing can be more charming than the view at sunset from this point, extending over the smiling and populous shores of the beautiful lake, to the distant peaks and glaciers of Glarus and of Uri. These become tinged with the most delicate pink by the distant rays of the sun, and present to the enraptured vision such a scene that no mortal painter could ever attempt to imitate. But Zurich, above all other things, lives in history, and will continue to live as long as history is read, for being the place where the Reformation commenced in Switzerland. In 1519 that bold and fearless man, Ulric Zwingli, began to denounce from the pulpit the sale of indulgences. He denounced the immoralities of the times, and necessarily raised around him a host of vindictive enemies. Like a patriot and a hero he breasted the storm for years. Civil war ensued. Swiss met Swiss on the bloody field of Cappel, and there this heroic divine fell, battle-axe in hand, with helmet on, his face to his God and his feet to his foe. The character of Ulric Zwingli is one on which the historian delights to dwell. With the simplicity of a child and the piety of a devoted Christian, he possessed all the learning of a ripe scholar, with the daring courage of a gallant soldier. He died at the early age of 47, and was emphatically a heroic leader of the " church militant."

While in Zurich I went to church (Sunday) and heard a sermon in German, from a distinguished professor in the university. The tones of the voice were often guttural, sometimes nasal, but never *musical*. Of course I could not understand a word the man said, but busied myself in noticing the manner in which the deacons of the church kept the boys and girls quiet. There were some three or four hundred in attendance, and as boys and girls will do, they kept up a constant " telegraphic snigger " with one another. During service these deacons, four in number, would be always on the move. If a boy was misbehaving, the first thing that would astonish his vision would be the stern face and staring eyes and bald head of the omnipresent deacon. This invariably made the youngster "dry up," and restored good order. I commend this to our own countrymen, for it is a most excellent plan to secure an orderly and quiet congregation of young people.

The Congress is now in session here, at my hotel, trying to fix up the peace of Villafranca. Liveried carriages are driving around, and diplomats are flitting about with the usual number of newsmongers and hangers on, all of which give this quiet town a decidedly gay and bustling appearance.

Adieu. I leave this evening, and will be to-morrow one of the pilgrims on the banks of the Rhine.

Yours truly,

H. W. A.

LETTER NO. XV.

Hotel de Russie, Baden-Baden,
August 31, 1859.

Editors Advocate:

Gentlemen—I arrived at this place on yesterday evening, and forthwith proceeded to take a bath, and then, as a matter of course, to bet a few Napoleon at Rouge et Noir. This is indeed a place to see sights. It is one vast "omnium gatherum" of all creation. It seems to me that all the ugly women and bald-headed men in Europe have assembled here to have a "kind of a show" of ugly faces and bald heads. The Ugly Club of Port Hudson is nothing compared to Baden-Baden at all, at all. The visitors are principally Germans and French, with a smart sprinkle of English and Americans. The improvements are good. The hotels, about a dozen in number, are very fine, with the most amiable and accommodating landlords. The waters of Baden have for centuries been visited for their healing qualities. A spring almost scalding hot issues from a mountain, and is conducted into an immense building with marble columns and fresco paintings, where the visitors daily assemble to drink the water. Here are long galleries for promenading in rainy weather.

But the great feature of Baden is its "conversation" or gambling saloon. This is an enormous palace, fitted up in the most gorgeous style, even with oriental luxuriance. Here are three large tables, two Rouge et Noir, or "Trente et Quarante," played with cards, and one roulette table. Men and women, old and young, assemble around these tables at 11 o'clock every day, and play without ceasing till one or two at night. Every thing is conducted in the most quiet and peaceable manner, the dealers and managers of the game being exceedingly accurate and expert in raking down the winnings and paying the losses. I saw one man frequently bet ten thousand francs "on the Rouge" and win it. Many, however, lose heavily, and render themselves miserable for life, often committing suicide. The company who own the bank, pays yearly $30,000 to the civil authorities of Baden, and at the same time has to expend a very large amount to furnish the establishment and keep the grounds in order. The "lady gamblers" here all have an air of abandon. They wear straw hats with feathers; some wear in their hats the entire plumage of the pheasant—all of which gives them a jaunty, sharp, knowing appearance, that is rather unpleasant to a man of my "retiring habits and excessive modesty."

We had a grand ball here to-night, which was of course very much crowded. The music was most excellent, the band being the Austrian Imperial. I do not think they dance as gracefully here as we do in Louisiana. The Austrian officers dance well, but carry themselves in a very stiff and ungraceful manner. Their coat-tails are entirely too short, which gives them the unpoetic appearance of "bobbing around." Among the ladies I saw but few pretty ones, the eternal Austrian pouting lips give them a coarse appearance—nearly all have red or flaxen hair, some even have yellow hair. In dress and style I think our American ladies are far ahead of any thing I have seen here—and as to beauty there is no comparison.

Baden is situated very much like the Sweet Springs of Virginia, in a beautiful valley. In the distance is the great Black Forest of Germany. Many wealthy persons have built themselves elegant cottages here, and come regularly every year to spend the summer. Every hotel is most beautifully decorated with vines and flowers, while the numerous walks over hill and dale are truly inviting to all who want delightful exercise. On my way here I stopped and spent a night in Strasbourg. Early in the morning I climbed to the top of the Cathedral, and took a good view of France, Switzerland, and Germany, then went back to my hotel, and ordered for breakfast a *Strasbourg pie.*

Last Sunday I spent "on the banks of Zurich's sweet waters." After going to church I took an excursion by steamer, to the head of Lake Zurich. It is a charming lake, and very thickly settled. It appears to be a continued village from one end of the lake to the other, while every foot of land seems to be planted in vines. Zurich is celebrated for having been the residence of the great reformer Zwingli, and the learned Lavater. They both died violent deaths—Zwingli was killed in battle, and Lavater was assassinated by a French soldier under Massena, during the battle of Zurich, in 1799. Zurich is the most enterprising and flourishing of all the Swiss Cantons. Here are extensive manufactories of silk and cotton goods, while the wines are very good. The library contains many old and interesting manuscripts. The arsenal is much resorted to, to see the identical cross-bow with which William Tell shot the apple from his son's head.

The Congress of the three powers, France, Austria, and Sardinia, is still in session in Zurich. They go very quietly to work, and discuss the affairs of Italy with closed doors. It is generally believed that its conclusions will be acquiesced in by all parties, and that peace and quiet will once more be restored.

Yours very truly,
H. W. A.

LETTER NO. XVI.

Hotel de la Rose,
Wiesbaden, Germany, *Sept.* 3, 1859.

Editors Advocate :

Gentlemen—I arrived here last evening from Frankfort-on-the-Main. The whole of Germany lies as it were "in a heap." Our friend, N. W. Pope, Esq., could take his cane and walk around one of their Duchies before breakfast. The city of Frankfort is a very pretty place, well located on the Main, and is one of the four free cities of Germany. It is a very old city, and has for many years been the centre of capital and money lenders, stocks, and stock-jobbers. Here the Rothschilds were born, and here they made the beginning of their immense fortune. This is also a kind of *entrepôt* for central Europe, receiving the productions and manufactures of all parts of the world, to be distributed in detail over the whole continent. Here are also many works of art. In a small museum built of marble and shaped like a Grecian temple, not like that built by our friend Moise, is the celebrated statue of "Ariadne by Dannecker." I have seen nothing in all my travels equal to it. It is very properly the boast of Frankfort, and draws crowds of visitors from all parts of Europe to see it. The statue is life-like—Ariadne is seated on a lioness, in a nude state. The features are after the highest order of classic art, while the body and limbs have all the luxurious plumpness of the Venus de Medicis.

In the Stadel Museum of pictures are some very fine paintings. Among them are two by Lessing, "the trial of John Huss," and the "Wise and Foolish Virgins," most admirable paintings. Frankfort was the birthplace of the great poet Goethe, and in one of the public squares stands his colossal statue by Schwantholar of Munich. Here also the celebrated Martin Luther, the great Reformer, lived. On his house there is the following Latin inscription: "*In silentio et spe erit fortitudo vestra.*"

The Jews are very numerous here, and command great influence as merchants and bankers. The Jewish maidens are very pretty, much the prettiest ladies that I have seen in all Germany. Their dark hair, the cold black liquid eye, the pensive but sweet face, bring back to my mind the Rebecca of Ivanhoe so beautifully described by Sir Walter Scott.

From Frankfort to this place, Wiesbaden, you pass through the small village of Hockheim, where the excellent wine of that name is made. It belongs to the Duke of Nassau, and yields him a large revenue in wines. The Rhine wines are very fine and exceedingly cheap. For instance you get a bottle of best Hockheimer here for two florins— that is about 80 cents—while the Vin Ordinaire of the country—very good table wine, and pure—can be had for 10 cents a bottle.

Wiesbaden is the capital of the Duchy of Nassau, and is the residence of the duke. It is remarkable for its hot baths, and is a great watering place on the same style as Baden-Baden. It is more frequented than any of the other German watering places, and may be called the Saratoga of this country. The Kursaal or gambling saloons are fitted up here with the most utter contempt of expense. It comes nearer the Pre Catalan at Paris than any other place I have yet seen. Here are colonades for walking in rainy weather, half a mile long, with fountains and flowers, serpentine walks up the mountains, and fishing in the Rhine. The gambling saloons are gorgeous in the extreme. There are six tables of Rouge et Noir. Around them an eager and impatient crowd is continually pressing to get an opportunity *to lose their money.* I saw an old, paralytic, gray-headed sinner, with one foot in the grave, betting with all the eagerness of a youth of nineteen. By his side stood a beautiful girl, seemingly not over seventeen, with jewelled fingers placing handfuls of Napoleons " on the Rouge."

The Duke of Nassau receives yearly the large sum of 43,000 florins for the license of this establishment, but at the same time prohibits by very severe penalties any of his subjects from betting at the banking games of Wiesbaden. He invites all foreigners to come and bet and spend their money freely, but will not permit his own people to do the same. Wise man that Duke!

In going to Frankfort I passed Heidelberg, where I spent several hours—visited the castle and the university, and took a delightful ride up the Neckar. The university has 700 students. Here you will recollect Jenny Lind was received in great state, and the hospitality of Heidelberg presented to her in a "tobacco box."

SUNDAY MORNING, COLOGNE, PRUSSIA.

Not having an opportunity of closing my letter at Wiesbaden on yesterday, I have deferred it till to-day. I took steamer yesterday morning at Biberich (the port for Wiesbaden) and arrived at this place last night.

The Rhine is a beautiful stream, about the size of Red River. It is very shallow in many places, and causes much delay in navigation during low water. Still up as high as Mayence small boats make regular trips. The great beauty of the Rhine scenery is the numerous castles which stud its banks, many of them now in very good repair. The vine is also here in the highest state of cultivation. I noticed in passing many high cliffs, that large baskets of earth were suspended and vines planted in them. A few miles from Mayence and near the village of Oestrich, is the celebrated chateau of Prince Metternich, called Johannisberg, of which you have often heard so much.

From this vineyard comes the far-famed Johannisberger wine, very much in demand with us. The chateau and vineyard are on the top of a high hill—a most romantic location. The vineyard contains only 70 acres, and averages about 160 casks per year. Thus you see we can't possibly get much from Johannisberg. The best of these wines are put away in the large cellars of the chateau, and the rest sold to whoever may wish to buy them. A few miles above, nearly adjoining, is the Steinberg chateau, where the Stein wines are made, almost equal to the Johannisberg. Thus, all along the Rhine are different chateaus, where different kinds of Rhine wines are made. I find, however, that the great majority of wines shipped to our country are bought up by the wholesale merchant, who mixes them (all pure wines) to suit color and taste—bottles and labels, and ships them abroad. It is very seldom, indeed, that a real pure bottle of Johannisberg wine reaches America. The wine may be the pure juice of the grape, but not from the Chateau Johannisberg.

Everybody talks Dutch here. A few moments ago a chubby-faced, red-cheeked chambermaid came into my room with a pitcher of hot water—for there being no barbers here, every man shaves himself: says I, "Parlez vous l'anglé?" Said she, "Yaw, hot wather." "D—n it," says I, "do you speak English?" "Yaw, yaw—goot hot wather!"

I had read Bulwer's Pilgrims of the Rhine, and remembered Byron's description:

> "The castled crags of Drachenfels
> Frown o'er the wide and winding Rhine,
> Whose breast of waters broadly swells
> Between the banks which bear the vine,
> And peasant girls with deep blue eyes
> Walk smilingly o'er this Paradise"—

but must confess that I am disappointed. To one fresh from the wild scenes of Switzerland the Rhine is tame and spiritless. There is much beauty, but little grandeur. The villages are picturesque, the castles interesting, as evidences of feudal power, and the river is a quiet tranquil stream of a pale green color, just such scenery as would please a love-sick maiden. But the grandeur of Mount Blanc is wanting—the rugged precipices of the Bay of Uri—the lofty mountains of Loch Lomond—even the Trosachs of Lake Katrine, are all far more sublime than any thing on the Rhine. Still tourists run crazy over the Rhine.

On the steamer coming down, were about 1,001 men and women, all with guide-books, and sketch-books, knapsacks and carpet-bags, and all "Pilgrims of the Rhine," determined to be charmed, determined to be delighted, determined to be enraptured. Says Miss Araminta Horsefly, (a languishing maid of sixteen,) "O mamma! do look at that nice old castle. Isn't it a love of a thing?" Lady Penelope Penfeather, (a very *spirituelle* widow,) "Oh, yes, it is charming—b-e-a-u-t-i-ful." There is a legend about the seven sisters who lived in that castle. A huge Dutchman here chimes in, "Yah, dat ish goot," while an English cockney, with a glass screwed into his eye, drawls out, "Yas, dem foin." I am sick of the Rhine. The boats are small and miserably constructed. In case it rains, unless you have an umbrella, you had better jump into the river at once in order to keep from getting wet.

On landing here, every thing is in confusion. Everybody is in everybody's way, keeping everybody as long as possible from getting everybody's baggage. If our friend Capt. Cotton would only run the Kenner or the Capitol up the Rhine with the stars and stripes, and learn these people something about the comforts and luxuries of an American steamer, I verily believe the travelling public would build him a monument on the "castled crags of Drachenfels."

Adieu. I am off to-night for Brussels and the field of Waterloo.

H. W. A.

LETTER NO. XVII.

Hotel Rubens, Antwerp, Belgium,
September 6, 1859.

Editors Advocate:

Gentlemen—I arrived at this place last night, and have spent the day in visiting the various churches, and studying the paintings of the great Rubens. This city was his home, and here are to be found his great master-pieces. In the Cathedral of Notre Dame is his "Descent from the Cross," and "The Crucifixion." The last is considered by artists to be one of the best paintings in the world. For great agony of expression in the dying thief, there is nothing like it. It is terribly frightful, so much so, that you involuntarily turn from it with a shudder. Rubens is almost deified in Belgium, and particularly in Antwerp. The Church of St. Jacques is the richest in marble sculpture and statuary of any in Belgium. Here is to be seen the altar-piece of Carrara marble brought by Rubens from Italy. In the museum are thirteen more of his paintings, all of them considered as great treasures, and which no money could buy. Here are also six original paintings by Van Dyck, most excellent specimens of this great master. He excels in portraits, while Rubens' great forte was in representing the dead body and the agony of the dying. When Napoleon took Belgium, the first thing he did was to seize these paintings, and carry them off to Paris, but after the battle of Waterloo, they were brought back and restored to their lawful owners. There are a great many private galleries of most excellent paintings in Antwerp, all rich in the works of the old masters. It seems that the moderns have lost the art (or rather have never found it) of great conception in painting—they also fail in the coloring. No modern artist has ever equalled the rich coloring of Rembrandt and Rubens, or the soft, silky touch of Murillo and Raphael.

The works of art are so rich and numerous in Antwerp, that a traveller could stay here for months. In the Church of St. Paul are the finest specimens of carving in oak—the pulpit is a wonderful triumph of a Jesuit's chisel. It represents Christ meeting the fishermen Peter and Andrew, all full size. The nets and fishes, the rocks and waves, the attitude of the fishermen, and the expression of the features of the Saviour, all are wonderfully given. In the museum of paintings is a very large painting by Frans Floris, (Flemish school,) called "The Descent of the Fallen Angels." On one of *these individuals* is painted a large fly, and it is so natural that hundreds have attempted, in passing, to " brush away that blue-tail fly." Attached to this same church is the representation of Mount Calvary, a very striking thing. An artificial hill is made of rock, and a crucifix with the Saviour placed on it. About 100 fine statues surround it. Death and the Serpent lie conquered at the foot of the cross.

Antwerp is quite a large place, having about 120,000 inhabitants. It is the commercial emporium of Belgium. Here are fine docks for shipping, and hundreds of sail and steamships leave here for all parts of the world. There is a fine line of steamers to New York.

The Scheldt is a quiet, sluggish river, very deep, and affords good navigation for the largest size vessels. The banks of the river are low, and the levees are high, which reminds me very much of the latitude of *West Baton Rouge*. I am now in the land of cabbages and wooden shoes. All the lower classes wear the sabot or clog, and such a pattering along the streets you never did hear. Still they all seem happy, and well-fed and contented. There are no beggars here, and but few loafers. The women are generally stout and strong, and work in the fields, and even on the railroad as laborers.

While at Cologne the other day, I visited the Church of St. Ursula, where I saw the bones of the 11,000 virgins who were murdered there by the Huns under Attila. I think I could have put those 11,000 virgins to a better use. I never saw such a "pile of bones" before. They are placed in every conceivable shape—they are even nailed up against the walls in the form of letters, and the name of many a saint is *spelled in bones.* In Cologne is the great Cathedral, the most remarkable perhaps in the world. It is now the largest, and its steeples, when completed, will be the tallest. In its immense aisles you are completely lost. I visited the Cathedral during high mass, and was very much entertained with the fine music. There is a huge organ, and also a full band of instrumental music, with a large number of singers, male and female.

A magnificent iron bridge has just been built over the Rhine at this place.

From Cologne I passed on to Aix-la-Chapelle. This is quite a city for summer resort. It contains hot springs and baths, which are much used by the people of Belgium. It also contains the cathedral in which was buried Charlemagne. His head and arms and legs (that is the bones) are still preserved in gold cases. Also are seen in this cathedral the many very valuable relics presented to Charlemagne by Harun al Raschid, the mighty Sultan. The sultan and Charlemagne were great friends, and their mutual admiration for each other seems to have been only equalled by their great liberality. The sultan sends his imperial brother a piece of the *true cross, a thorn from the crown,* and the *veritable girdle of the Saviour*—all of these are set in gold and precious stones, making the most splendid array of barbaric magnificence I ever saw.

From Aix I went to Brussels, where I spent yesterday. Brussels is a very American-looking place, with nice streets and fine parks. It is full of monuments and statues, some of them very fine. It also has the fine manufactories of lace, for which it is more particularly known by the ladies of our country. I visited the factories, and saw the most beautiful articles being made. It is all done by hand. The thread is made at Valenciennes from the common flax, and sells for more than its weight in gold.

But Brussels is close to Waterloo, and hence thousands visit it to see the great battle-field where the giants fought. The village of Waterloo is twelve miles from Brussels, and lies in a beautiful rolling country, well suited for a great battle. On the battle-field is a huge mound of earth 225 feet high, and surmounted by an immense stone statue of the Belgic Lion, who looks towards France with a bold and triumphant look. This statue is particularly offensive to all Frenchman. Indeed, a Frenchman seldom comes to Waterloo. In 1830, when the French troops were marching through Brussels on to Holland, a French soldier went up to the lion on the Waterloo monument, and broke *his majesty's tail into three pieces!* He was detected in attempting to blow up the whole concern, and arrested by the authorities, who keep a guard there now to protect it.

The Belgians speak French. It is their national language. I attended the sitting of the Senate, which is now in session, and heard several speeches, all in French. They read their speeches, as many of our senators do, but do not imitate the Americans in length, theirs being always very short.

THE HAGUE, HOLLAND, *Sept.* 8.

I could not close my letter at Antwerp, but came on by railway to Delft, and thence by steamer to Rotterdam—thence to this place. Delft is an ancient place. We know it in our country principally from its giving the name to our common earthenware. The extensive manufacture of pottery has in a great measure ceased. Here Grotius, the great law writer, was born. Also here William I., Prince of Orange, was assassinated. A few miles farther on is Rotterdam, the second city in Holland. It is a queer-looking place. Every street has its canal. Boats, even large ships, are seen in the very heart of the city. The dogs here take the place of horses, and it is astonishing what immense loads they can pull. The whole country is much lower than the sea—protected by immense levees or dykes, as they call them here. Dogs, dykes, and windmills are great institutions in Holland. Still the women are pretty, right down pretty. They all look fresh and clean, and healthy. True they have broad flat feet and round chubby faces, and can't say a word, but the eternal yaw—yaw—still, I like the Dutch gals.

Adieu, my dear sirs. I leave to-day for the mouth of the Rhine, to examine the huge locks and dams that the Dutch engineers have built, in order to *scour out* the channel of this great European Mississippi.

Truly yours,
H. W. A

LETTER NO. XVIII.

Amsterdam, Holland, *Sept.* 9, 1859.

Editors Advocate:

I have just finished, after a hard day's labor, the examination of the locks at the mouth of the Rhine, and the huge pumps or water-works at Haarlem Lake. They are both immense works, and to a Louisianian full of interest. The locks were finished under the reign of Louis Bonaparte; since the restoration, however, the very name of Bonaparte has been erased, and the chief engineer's placed in its stead. For many centuries the Rhine, in emptying its waters into the North Sea, had overflowed an immense country at its mouth; just as the Mississippi does at present. The Dutch came to the conclusion that it was best to tap the Rhine near its mouth, and thus let off its surplus waters, and at the same time carry off the rain-water which was doing them great damage. For this purpose they have dug a huge canal, and constructed three locks across it, which opens to the

Rhine and shuts against the sea. When the tide is high the gates are shut, when it is low they are open. This canal is 300 feet wide, and 20 feet deep, and 25 miles long!

But the great work of Holland is the reclaiming of Haarlem Lake. This was a lake of water 20 miles long, and containing an area of 45,000 acres. They went to work and built a levee around this lake 15 feet high, and then started three huge draining machines, each machine working eleven monster pumps, six feet in diameter! They kept all these pumps going for *four years*, when the very bottom of the lake became dry land. The land was sold at a very high price, and the draining machines are still kept up at an annual tax of about 50 cents per acre. It is now a rich and flourishing country, with handsome dwellings and splendid farms, where the salt sea once remained supreme. From the tower or observatory of the huge draining machine, you can see almost to Amsterdam, a distance of 30 miles. Land that was once covered with water, is now worth 500 guilders per acre, while smiling plenty is seen on every hand. The soil reclaimed is peculiarly rich, and commands a much higher price than other lands.

Last night I spent in the Hague. It is the capital of Holland, and full of interesting reminiscences. The streets are narrow but clean, and the houses generally built of brick, covered with the Dutch tile. The churches of Holland have all been stripped of their paintings and statuary.

They present cold, damp walls, and remind one of the days of William of Orange.

I stopped to-day at Leyden, and spent the day. In the town-hall are many fine paintings, one particularly that is known to history. It is "The Last Judgment," by Lucas of Leyden, over four hundred years old, and still the coloring is good, and the painting considered one of the very best of the old masters. In this great painting, hell is represented on the left, and a legion of devils are engaged in pulling and driving the wicked into eternal torment, while a huge devil is pushing a beautiful woman into the mouth of the fiery dragon, with a pitchfork. The burgomaster of the town was very polite, and opened the doors of the galleries without pay or reward. This is the first collection of paintings that I have seen in Europe without paying for it.

The Dutch are a very persevering, industrious people. The ride from the Hague to Leyden is a delightful one. You pass through an immense forest, all planted by the present generation, and since the land has been reclaimed from the sea. There are also many very elegant private residences, surrounded with flowers and fountains, and all that art could suggest or wealth buy.

Amsterdam is a large city; it has over 200,000 inhabitants. Here are all nations of the world assembled. It is the northern Venice of Europe. Hundreds of families live in boats and die in boats. The streets are like Rotterdam, that is, a canal for every street. The Jews are very numerous, and have great influence as bankers and jewellers. This is the only city that manufactures the smalt used so extensively in painting on porcelain; also borax is very extensively made here. Here also are the lapidaries, who grind the precious stones and cut the diamonds. In the museum are many fine paintings; among them is one by Vander Helst, called "The Miracle of Holland." It is a very large painting, containing twenty-five portraits, all true to life, and most admirably done. These are considered by artists to be the best portraits in the world. The palace is an immense building, and is the spring residence of the king. It is finished in the most gorgeous and elaborate style with marble carvings. The ball-room is 180 feet long and 90 feet wide, and 100 feet to the ceiling. The entire room, sides, roof, floor, and all, is composed of pure Carrara marble. Well may the Dutch be proud of this, their greatest work of art, for there is nothing superior to it in all Europe.

The cholera has been very fatal of late in Belgium and Holland, and has carried off hundreds and thousands of all classes.

To a Louisianian, Holland is an exceedingly interesting country. Here you find a people, who for centuries have been fighting great battles against their greatest enemy, the sea. They have often suffered very much, occasionally whole villages being swept away. Still they have not been discouraged, but have rallied under the severest misfortunes—built their levees higher, and given them more base, and now rest secure from the waves of the "stormy sea." Year after year they taxed themselves, and built levee after levee, until at last they have triumphed. The levees are under the entire control of the General Government. A corps of engineers are kept always engaged in watching and repairing them. By this means Holland is to-day one of the most prosperous and happy countries in Europe.

We have only the Mississippi to levee. This can be done effectually. In Holland they have fought and conquered the Rhine and the Ocean. We should then take courage in Louisiana—change our entire levee system—place it under the control of the State, and make it the duty of the Commissioner of Public Works to take charge of all levees, from the Balize to the Arkansas line. Give them full power to construct, rebuild, and repair all levees at the expense of the general levee fund, and then we will have no more overflows.

Good-bye. I leave to-day for Berlin.

Yours, very truly,

H. W. A.

LETTER NO. XIX.

Berlin, Hotel du Nord, *Sept.* 11, 1859.

Editors Advocate:

This is a great city, full of works of art, men of science, and regal splendor. It is one of the largest capitals of Europe, having a population of nearly half a million of inhabitants. The great number of soldiers here gives to Berlin almost the air of a camp. Every morning at 11 o'clock they "mount guard" in true military style. A splendid band of music plays, and 10,000 troops go through their military evolutions, and defile before you to their several stations in and around the city. The river Spree, a small and sluggish stream about the size of the Tickfaw, runs through the city, and communicates with the Oder and the Baltic on the one hand, and empties into the Elbe on the other. The situation of Berlin is low and sandy, in the midst of a dreary plain. It is surprising that the foundation of a town should have been laid on so uninteresting a spot; but it is far more surprising that it should have grown up, notwithstanding, into the flourishing capital of a great empire. Owing to the want of stone in the neighborhood, the largest portion of the buildings are made of brick and plaster. This gives to the city a sameness, as if the great Frederick had given out the building of the entire city by contract. Edinburgh, or London, or Paris, all have many evidences of antiquity, but Berlin looks as if every house in it was plastered the same day. The good people of Boston and Vicksburg complain bitterly of their high hills and uneven streets. In this city they complain equally as much of their *deadlevel* location and stagnant gutters. The Friedrichstrasse is two miles long. There is not a foot of descent from one end of it to the other.

Notwithstanding the disadvantages of situation, Berlin is certainly one of the finest cities in Europe. Few great cities can show so much architectural splendor as is seen in the colossal Palace, the beautiful and classic Museum, the chaste Guard House, the great Opera, and the University opposite. These, with the Arsenal, the finest specimen of "warlike architecture" in the world, and the University, are all within a stone's throw of each other, and can be seen alternately by turning on one's heel. Most of these elegant buildings are situated on the great street called Unter der Linden, (under the linden tree,) from a double row of linden or lime trees, which form a shady walk in the centre, while on each side is a carriage-way. It is the principal and most magnificent street in the city. The view along it is terminated by the Brandenburg gate, a splendid affair, and one of the great ornaments of the city. It was built in 1792, and is an imitation of the Propylæum at Athens, but on a larger scale. The car of victory on the top of the gate, was carried to Rome as a trophy by Napoleon, but it was recovered by the Prussians after the battle of Waterloo, who bestowed upon the goddess (the figure) after her return, the eagle and iron cross which she now bears.

The Prussians not only appear to be great artists, but are exceedingly patriotic, for they have almost crowded their streets and public squares with statues and monuments to their great benefactors. To their King Frederick the Great, they have recently erected the most magnificent statue, or rather group of statues, I ever beheld. It is by their great sculptor Rauch, (pronounced Rowk,) and is the grandest monument in the wide world. It is built in the centre of the Unter der Linden, opposite the University, and consists of a granite pedestal 25 feet high, presenting on each face bronze groups of the great commanders of the Seven Years' War, on foot and horseback, all the size of life, and all portraits in high relief.

Among the distinguished persons represented here are the Duke of Brunswick, afterwards the commander of the allies against Dumouriez, Prince Heinrich of Prussia, Generals Seydlitz and Zeithen, Counts von Finckenstein and von Carmer, Graun,

Lessing, and Kant—the whole number on the four faces of the pedestal being 31. To reproduce these correctly, the best authorities have been consulted, and authentic drawings, busts, and medals of the period have been strictly followed. This, as a matter of course, has involved an immense amount of labor, but the value of the monument as an historical work, is thereby increased tenfold. The costumes and arms of the time are given with equal accuracy. Above, there is at each corner a female figure, representing the four cardinal virtues—Prudence, Justice, Fortitude, and Temperance. Between them are bas-reliefs emblematic of different periods of the monarch's life. In the first is represented his birth and education, civil and military. In the second relief, a muse is teaching the young prince history; pointing out to him the names of the commanders he most admired—Alexander, Cæsar, and Gustavus Adolphus. In the third, Minerva is giving him a sword. In the fourth, the great king is represented after his defeat at Kolin, sitting down, and looking earnestly on the ground, on which he is drawing the lines of a plan with his cane. This subject is familiar to every German.

In the back-ground of the tablet are allegorical figures of Triumph and Victory, intimating that the defeat was retrieved. The other reliefs represent him as encouraging the arts of peace. Now in the hut of a Silesian weaver—now playing on his flute, or walking in the gardens of "Sans-souci." From the centre of this group rises the monarch himself, seated on horseback. This statue is 17 feet 3 inches high, and although colossal, it is in such beautiful proportion that its great size is toned down in a wonderful manner. The horse is poised in a trotting position, with two feet raised. The long walking-cane, the three-cornered hat, the pistol holsters, are all copied minutely from the relics of the great king. I have thus been perhaps tedious in the description of this grand monument. It is the greatest triumph of the greatest artist since the days of Michael Angelo, and is well worth a trip across the Atlantic to see it.

Rauch is but recently dead. He has also left behind him many other statues which have immortalized his name. Among them are his "King Frederick and Louisa," in marble, at Charlottenburg. The museum at Berlin is, however, the "great lion" of the city. It has just been entirely remodelled. A long row of pillars now fronts the Unter den Linden, and a magnificent new building has been added to the main edifice. The great Cornelius, the best fresco painter now living, has for years given his whole time and talents towards ornamenting this splendid structure. The walls of the colonnade, and the ceilings of the interior, are covered with classic works, by the best living painters. The museum is the pride of the city, and is under the direction of the government. It contains on the ground floor the Antiquarium; on the second the Sculpture Gallery, and on the third floor the Picture Gallery. Among the antique statuary is "The Boy Praying," found in the bed of the Tiber. It is of bronze, and is one of the very best specimens of antique art. The picture gallery is divided into numerous small compartments, with appropriate labels over each apartment, describing the pictures, and giving the names of their authors. The Berlin Gallery does not rank so high as those of Dresden and Munich, in works of first-rate excellence, but it has good specimens of a great number of masters of the early German and Italian schools. Raphael has one or two paintings here, after his best style. Titian and Andrea del Sarto are also fully represented. Murillo, and Carlo Dolce, and Guido are also to be seen on the canvased walls; but the pride of this gallery is the large number of German and Dutch paintings of the highest order. Lucas Cranach and Hans Holbein may be called the fathers of the German school. They lived in the days of Martin Luther. Many of their paintings are now as fresh as if the colors were mixed on yesterday.

Lessing, the great German artist, is here seen in all his glory. His great painting of the "Burning of John Huss," is now in the Dusseldorf Gallery at New York. Here is his "Trial of Huss," and many other pieces which have given him immortality. In this gallery I noticed a fine picture by an artist not known to fame, but in portrait painting the best I ever saw. It is Balthazar Denner, a Dutch painter. It is the portrait of an old man, and cost $10,000. I have never seen such details in any picture. The color of the eyes is perfect; every freckle, every crow's-foot and wrinkle are as well defined as if the living man was before you. Here also I noticed a painting of great merit by Von Laeck, another Dutchman. It seemed to attract great attention, and I, in company with some English ladies, walked up to look at it. It was "Venus smacking the back of Cupid." The goddess seemed angry, and was laying on with might and main, while the little rascal was red with spanking, and seemed to be crying at the top of his lungs.

The University of Berlin stands deservedly among the very first of Europe. As a medical school it ranks the first in Germany, and has 1,500 students. Here are students from all parts of the world, many from the United States. Jena, and Bonn, and Heidelburg are all fine institutions, but Berlin possesses many advantages over all, Vienna not excepted.

The Arsenal, (Zenghaus,) a building of faultless architecture, was erected in 1695. Above the windows, round the inner court, are 22 masks, admirably carved in stone, by Schlüter, representing the human face in the agonies of death. On the ground floor are cannon and artillery of various kinds. On the second floor are ranged 100,000 stand of arms. Here are also a great many curious old guns of every age, used when gunpowder was first invented. Here also are seven bunches of keys, of various fortresses, taken by Prussian arms. Also 1,000 stand of colors, mostly taken from the French, at Paris, in 1815.

Berlin has not many very fine churches; the most remarkable is the Cathedral, (Dom.) It is the burial place of the royal family, and contains the remains of many sovereigns in gilded coffins. I travelled all night from Amsterdam to this city, expressly to hear the "Berlin Choir" sing the Mendelssohn psalms, unaccompanied by instrumental music. I arrived in time Sunday morning, and repaired to the cathedral, where I was well repaid for my long night's journey. The sermon was preached in German, (all of which was *Dutch* to me,) but the music was most admirable. It was far superior to any chorus at any opera I had ever heard.

The manufactories of Berlin are very great. Iron, copper, and bronze are manufactured here into a thousand different articles. China-ware, glass, jewelry, musical instruments, mathematical and astronomical instruments, boots, shoes, and woollen goods—all these articles are manufactured in a very superior manner, and give employment to thousands of operatives.

Berlin also excels in works of "high art"— painting and statuary. Here are found the studios of the great German living masters.

Immediately beyond the Brandenburg gate commences the Park, (Thiergarten.) It is a lovely spot, containing 500 acres of land, and is shaded by tall trees, interspersed with groups of shrubbery. Here and there are open spaces for ponds and statuary, and elegant romantic coffee-houses. The Prussians have made this an earthly paradise. Here are beautiful walks and delightful drives, and "rotten rows," with statues and fountains and flowers interspersed.

Potsdam is the Versailles of Berlin. It is about 25 miles distant by rail, and is a small place, being only remarkable for its palaces, and the gardens of "Sans-souci." These grounds are very elegantly laid off, and extend for many miles in every direction. The Palace of Charlottenburg, in these gardens, is a most remarkable pile of marble and gilt. It was built by Frederick the Great, after his long wars were over, in order to show the world that he was not *entirely broke*. Money has been squandered here in every conceivable manner. Such a profusion of mosaics, tortoise-shell, alabaster, malachite, amber, and lapis lazuli was never seen before. The visitor is required to take off his shoes, and put on felt slippers, in walking through the apartments of this palace, for the floors are all of the finest mosaics.

The old king still lives at "Sans-souci." Poor old man! He is in a dying condition. His disease is softening of the brain, brought on by drinking too much Cliquot champagne! for he was *no one-bottle* man, but a good honest drinker! His palace, although surrounded by all the trappings of royalty, looks cold and dreary. The solitary sentinel paces slowly in front of the door, while none enter except his physician or the next of kin. His *faithful* subjects pass by, and crack their jokes about *old Cliquot*, as they call him, with (I think) great irreverence!

"Weary lies the head that wears a crown." Yes, this poor old king seems to have a hard time of it, without even the sympathy of his people, for he never had their affections.

In the Garrison Kirche (Church of the Garrison) are the remains of the great Frederick, in a plain zinc coffin. It looks like a box of sheet-iron, and in no manner like the sarcophagus of a great monarch. Over this coffin are suspended the eagles and standards taken from Napoleon's armies at Leipsic and Waterloo, in order to appease the manes of Frederick, whose sword had been taken from his tomb by Napoleon, and carried off to Paris; a fitting atonement to the shade of the old hero for this paltry theft. I noticed on the terraced gardens of "Sans-souci," our ordinary pumpkin planted, and the vines trailed along, with the ripe red and yellow fruit hanging very artistically down the terraces, making our democratic vegetable not only useful but ornamental. "A dainty dish to set before a king."

I called on our Minister, Gov. Wright, who was very kind and attentive to me. Our talented young friend, Ed. Butler, of Iberville, is attached to this legation. He gave me a real Louisianian welcome, and made my stay in Berlin very agreeable. We went to the grand opera together, and witnessed the performance of an extraordinary ballet, which is now all the rage in Berlin. Our young friend stands very high here in diplomatic circles, and is destined to be a prominent man in our State. Success to him, for he is as clever a fellow as ever lived.

For many years Berlin has been the residence of many men of great scientific attainments. Among them were the celebrated Alexander von Humboldt, a name known in every land, and honored by all. Kings and emperors were proud to have him as an associate, while this truly great man looked with contempt on all the honors they showered upon him. He died very recently, and lies buried a few miles from the city. His grave is visited by all lovers of science, and his memory is revered by prince and people.

Adieu. I leave to-morrow for Dresden.

Very truly yours,

H. W. A.

LETTER NO. XX.

Victoria Hotel, Dresden, Saxony,
Sept. 15, 1859.

Editors Advocate:

I reached this old but very interesting city in six hours from Berlin—distance 116 miles—fare 110 silbergroshens, or about $3. Saxony has for many years played a very important part in the history of the world, and its capital was often the scene of terrible conflicts of contending armies. During the Seven Years' War, Frederick the Great besieged this city, and in later times Napoleon I. came to its relief, while surrounded by the troops of the Allies. It was on this memorable occasion that Gen. Moreau was killed. This great general, who had immortalized himself at the battle of Hohenlinden, was now with the allied sovereigns. The beleaguering forces extended all round the old town, from the barrier of Pirna on the Elbe, to the marsh of Preisnitz. Near the small village of Racknitz stood a group of mounted officers, on the

27th day of August, 1813. At the command of Napoleon they were fired on, he saying "that he suspected there were some *small generals* among them." The first shot took effect—Moreau fell. Both legs, which were cut off by a cannon ball, are buried here. A large square block of granite, surmounted by a helmet, has been erected on the spot where he received his mortal wound, with this inscription: "Moreau, the hero, fell here, by the side of Alexander, 27th August, 1813." His body was conveyed to St. Petersburg, and buried there in great state. The distance of the shot was so great, that Napoleon had it accurately measured, and found it to be exactly 2,000 yards—about a mile and a quarter. Napoleon III. did much better shooting than that at the battle of Solferino. At three miles he did good work with his rifle cannon.

Dresden is situated on the Elbe, a clear and romantic stream, about two or three hundred yards wide. It has been called the "German Florence." Its delightful situation, its fine collection of rare and elegant paintings, its statuary and its jewels, I should think would make it compare favorably with the great Italian city. I find many Americans here, with their children at school. They tell me that in music and the modern languages, Dresden has great advantages. For ages, the china of this place has been in much demand. Its porcelain manufactories are still carried on to a great extent, while the painting on china seems to have taken rank among the lovers of "high art."

But the pride of Dresden is her gallery of paintings. This alone brings thousands to Saxony, from all parts of the world. When the great Napoleon robbed all Europe of its paintings, not even excepting the Vatican at Rome, he spared this gallery, and seemed to take a great delight in visiting it. Frederick, while bombarding the city, ordered his engineers to save the gallery of paintings. He battered down walls, and churches, and palaces. He entered Dresden as a conqueror, but asked permission of the captive monarch to visit this gallery as a stranger, so much did he esteem these paintings. Among the 2,000 paintings exhibited here, I have not room to describe but two or three. The first in the gallery, and perhaps the best painting out of Italy, is the celebrated "Madonna di San Sisto," by Raphael. The sainted Pope Sixtus, from whom the picture is named, is represented on the one side, gazing with pious and trembling awe upon the figure of the Virgin, who is soaring up to heaven, in all the majesty with which the Roman Catholic religion has surrounded her, bearing in her arms the divine Child. The head of the Virgin is perhaps nearer the perfection of female beauty than any thing on canvas. It is truly impressive and beautiful. Opposite to the pope kneels St. Barbara; her youthful beauty and fervor contrast most admirably with his aged form. Below this group are two angelic children, their countenances beaming with intelligence and pure innocence. With eyes upturned to the central figures of the picture, they are the happiest effort of the great artist. This picture was purchased from a convent at Piacenza for 17,000 ducats, about $40,000, and is now considered more valuable than all the jewels in "the crown the Bourbon lost." An elegant apartment is appropriated to this great painting, and there you may recline on the sofas from morning till night, with nothing to interrupt the pleasant reverie produced by a close study of this great work of art. There is, perhaps, no painting more generally copied, and more numerously distributed through the Christian world. In the world of art it ranks only second to "The Transfiguration," in the Vatican at Rome.

The next great painting is the "La Notte," by Correggio. This is considered the master-piece of this great Italian, and all the powers of his art are here united to make it a perfect work. It is a representation of the Madonna and Child, and is called "Notte," (night,) because it represents the Mother and Child in a dark room, and the only light produced is from the supernatural halo emitted from the infant Saviour. The effect is truly astonishing. The Virgin mother, who bends over the Infant, is undazzled, while another female draws back, veiling her eyes with her hand, as if unable to endure the radiance. Far off through the gloom of night we see the morning just breaking along the eastern horizon, emblem of the "Day-spring from on high." Correggio did not, like Rembrandt, in these effects attempt to give the color of lamp-light. The emitting the light from the child, though a supernatural illusion, is eminently successful; it looks neither forced nor improbable. In the adaptation of light and shadow to the illusion of the subject, it is certainly one of the greatest triumphs of modern art. These two are the gems of the gallery. There are many other paintings of rare excellence, by the old masters. Rubens and Titian, Dosso Dossi and Guido, Paul Veronese and Andrea del Sarto, Girard Dow and Albert Durer, Holbein, Paul Potter, Rembrandt, Van Dyck, and Teniers, are all here represented by their master-pieces of the "divine art."

The next great curiosity in Dresden is the "Green Vault," in which are large suites of rooms filled with curiosities, articles of *virtu*, gold and silver plate, and precious jewels. For many years the kings of Saxony drew immense revenues from their silver mines at Freiburg, and they all seem to have had a strange fancy in spending their money in the purchase of what might very properly be called an immense curiosity-shop. I saw many rare jewels in this vault, of surpassing beauty: the diamond decorations of the elector, consisting of buttons, collar, sword-hilt and scabbard, all of diamonds of great size. The three brilliants in the epaulette weigh 50 carats each. But the most remarkable stone of all is the *green brilliant*, weighing 160 grains! considered the finest of the kind in the world. These treasures are contained in eight apartments, each exceeding the previous one in the splendor and richness of its contents. In one of these apartments I noticed "The Fall of Lucifer and the Wicked Angels," cut out of one block or piece of ivory, containing 142 figures; two goblets composed entirely of cut gems, valued each at 30,000 francs; a chimney-piece of Dresden china, sparkling with precious stones; "The Court of the Great Mogul," represented in pure gold, valued at $60,000. These are a few of the rare and costly trinkets seen here.

The armory is in the "Zwinger," a large public building, and contains the most perfect specimens of armor now in existence; far superior to the Tower at London. Here you pass, for 100 yards or more, through long files of mounted knights, with steel-clad armor, their visors down, and lances in rest, seemingly ready for the charge. Two of these tilting suits of armor deserve particular notice. They each weigh 200 pounds, and are finished in the most classic and elaborate style. The surface is covered with reliefs, representing the labors of Hercules, the Golden Fleece, and Theseus and Ariadne, all evincing the hand of the master artist. In another apartment I saw the little cocked hat of Peter the Great, and the boots which Napoleon wore at the battle of Dresden. Here also is a specimen of pure silver, taken from the Freiburg mines; it is large enough and has been used for the elector's dinner-table. Here also is a great curiosity, the only one I ever saw of the kind —it is a long tube, formed by lightning falling on a bed of sand, which has been partially melted by the electric fluid, wherever it took its course, and thus has made " a hollow rope of sand."

Dresden has an old appearance. It is a very quiet place. The sound of the hammer or the buzz of the machine-shop is never heard. Its principal manufactories seem to be in porcelain and musical instruments. The arts flourish here, particularly the art of painting on china, in which they greatly excel all other places. There are but few fine churches. The court church, between the bridge and the palace, is not by any means an imposing building. It is, however, decorated in all the gorgeous drapery of the Italian style.

The royal family profess the Catholic religion, though their subjects are Lutherans. Augustus II., as the price of obtaining the crown of Poland, abjured the Protestant religion, of which his ancestors had been the earliest and most faithful supporters. The two religions seem to be getting along very well together. There does not appear to be any jealousy between them. The large mass of the German people are free-thinkers. They read the ponderous works of Immanuel Kant, and drink oceans of lager-bier. Thus fortified, they are ready to dispute with St. Peter himself, or chop logic with John Bunyan, John Calvin, John Wesley, or John Hughes.

Few European capitals contain a greater number of objects calculated to gratify the curiosity of the intelligent traveller. It is the residence of many men of learning and talent, who contribute much to make society agreeable. The opera is good, and music is much cultivated. The climate is generally mild and agreeable, while food and lodging are not dear. It is now much resorted to by English and Americans, for education and economy. It has neither fine streets nor imposing public buildings, but its situation is pretty, and its environs really delightful. The terrace of Bruhl runs along the left bank of the Elbe, and forms a delightful promenade. On this terrace are two very elegant cafés, the "Reale" and the "Belvidere," where the *elite* of Dresden are seen every evening. Besides these, there are numerous fine "lagerbier" saloons. The beer here is very good. I much prefer it to the cheap wines of the country.

Last night I went to the opera, and heard the comic piece of "Herr Pantalon," or "Good-night, Mr. Simmons." It was well given by the best artists of the city. Whether this opera was written in consequence of the retiring from politics of our old friend from Iberville, I know not; but the music was good, and the principal male singer reminded me very much of the broad proportions of my old Democratic friend, who always carried much *weight* in our legislative deliberations.

We get nothing from Dresden but china-ware and musical instruments. China-ware, or porcelain, was originally brought from the country after which it is named, and was first made in Europe at this place in 1710, by one Botticher, an alchemist, who, after wasting a great deal of the gold of his patron, Augustus I. of Poland, in his search for the philosopher's stone, stumbled by accident on a more sure method of producing the precious metals, by the discovery of an art which has served to enrich his countrymen. The Dresden china is not so valuable as the Sèvres. It is, however, more durable, and much better adapted to practical use. It graces the tables of all the crowned heads of Europe, and is much sought after by the wealthy aristocracy of every land.

Adieu. I leave for Vienna to-morrow, in which great city I expect to be " a quiet looker-on " for a few days.

Truly your friend,
H. W. A.

LETTER NO. XXI.

Hotel l'Agneau d'Or, Vienna, Austria,
Sept. 18, 1859.

Editors Advocate :

I have the pleasure to write you to-day from the banks of the " dark-rolling Danube." From Dresden to this city is 18 hours by rail. The road passes through Saxon-Switzerland, Bohemia, and Moravia. At Prague I took breakfast, and spent an hour in examining the Bohemian ware so much prized in our country, and in fact all over the world where good taste is cultivated and good wine drank. It is mostly manufactured in the city of Prague, this being the principal employment of its inhabitants. In the manufactories here I saw a beautiful article, the "wine cooler," made of frosted glass. It is really very beautiful, and will be a great ornament to the dining-table.

Prague is a large city, with a population of 150,000 inhabitants, and is beautifully situated on the banks of the Moldau, in a lovely valley, surrounded by romantic hills. Here was fought, once upon a time, a certain great battle, many years ago, with the music of which our school-misses are pretty well acquainted, for I verily believe that the "Battle of Prague" and "Days of Absence" were the first two pieces of music I ever heard on the piano. Bohemia is a beautiful, undulating country, and reminds me very much of the lands around Huntsville in North Alabama. Here the grasses, buckwheat, rye, and Indian corn flourish well, and yield large crops.

Between Prague and Vienna are large pastures covered with thousands of sheep and cattle. The shepherds dress in a very romantic style, and are always seen in the midst of their flocks. I saw a great many Gypsies on the roadside in their rude tents, but did not see the "Bohemian Girl," of whom we all have heard so much in poetry and in song. These Gypsies form a large portion of the population of Bohemia. They are still nomadic, and wander about from place to place, mending a few tin-pans, stealing a little grain, and occasionally a child of some wealthy man, and then restoring it again for a large reward. The Austrian government seems to deal gently with these "children of the woods." They are permitted to roam wherever they please, and pitch their tents in field or forest. During the summer months they establish quite extensive villages on the banks of the Moldau, and live on fish and fowl. The women tell fortunes, and sing and dance; while the men are idle, lazy vagabonds, too proud to beg, but perfectly willing to steal. They keep up their nationality, and pride themselves on their ancestors, of whom they of course know but little. It is generally believed they came from Hindostan, but that they may all go to the d—l, seems to be the pious wish of every civilized community, where the rights of "meum and tuum" are acknowledged. The men are generally dark-featured and ungainly, but the women are often very pretty. With dark raven hair and coal-black eyes, they have often captivated men of rank and fortune, and even princes of royal blood. The romantic novelist and the crack-brained bard have ever had a penchant for the Gypsy. The Gypsy hat and the Gypsy dress have attracted the attention of the French milliners, while the "Queen of the Gypsies" has been the object of envy for many a bread-and-butter school-miss, who sighed for red scarfs, and bare feet, and running brooks. The Gypsy lives in story and in song, and has been the heroine of many a delightful opera.

But here we are in Vienna. It is very pleasantly situated on the Danube, and contains a population of 450,000 inhabitants. It looks more like Paris than any European city I have seen. The streets are wide and well paved, and the cabmen, with fine horses, drive up and down the thoroughfares like so many Jehus. The Danube is about the size of the Ohio, but much deeper. It is navigated by a great many steamers, making regular trips to various ports, but all of them small and very uncomfortable. Vienna is remarkable for its coffee-houses, for here it was that this *great institution* began. The cafés are generally kept by the girls of Vienna. They are really beautiful, dress very neatly, and present you with a cup of coffee in a very smiling and graceful manner. These establishments are fitted up in the most gorgeous and costly manner, and are the resort of the gay and fashionable of the city. I saw this evening in the Café Leopoldstadt a sight that is not usually seen in any other European city. A richly dressed Greek was sipping his coffee with a "turbaned Turk," while a Cossack and an Austrian soldier were smoking their meerschaums with one of the "tribe of Barabbas."

The fare is very good in Vienna, but I do not like the Austrian wine. Tokay is drank very freely here. I cannot bear it. Its taste is too aromatic, and gives to the mind the unpleasant idea of its being drugged or medicated. It is made in Hungary out of the white grape, and is much esteemed by the bon vivants of Austria. To bring on the "board" a bottle of "Imperial Tokay," is considered in Austria the highest mark of hospitality to the invited guest.

In Vienna, the Croat and the Bohemian, the Moravian and the Dalmatian, the Hungarian and the Venetian, all meet, dressed in their peculiar costumes, which give to this city a very gay and picturesque appearance. The Turks visit this city in great numbers, and carry on an immense trade. This is in every respect the most oriental city in Christian Europe, except Moscow. Its trade with the Black Sea is very great, and its communication now with Constantinople and the East almost direct.

I spent yesterday in the picture galleries and the arsenal. The paintings are very fine, particularly in the gallery of Prince Lichtenstein. It is astonishing what immense fortunes seem to have accumulated in the hands of private persons in this country. In the United States, when a man gets to be worth a million of dollars, we call him rich; but here are numbers of the aristocracy of Austria worth from fifty to one hundred millions each. This magnificent gallery, the Lichtenstein, occupying an immense palace, is valued at several millions pounds sterling. In it are over two thousand paintings, many of them by the best masters, and all good specimens of this great art. I saw here the greatest profusion of Rubens and Van Dyck, I have yet seen out of Belgium. Rubens is a coarse and florid painter. He portrays the passions very well, and is great in crucifixions and death scenes, but will not compare with the great Italian masters in his madonnas or other pieces of repose and devotion. I have thus far seen but two or three of Raphael's pictures. They are really divine, and to my humble judgment far superior to any thing of Rubens at Antwerp or the Hague.

In the Imperial Arsenal I saw the *rifled cannon* taken by the Austrians from the French at the battle of Solferino. It is a handsome brass gun, and from it the Austrians have already made a great many of a similar kind, and of a larger calibre. This French gun has six rifles, and did good execution at a distance of three miles, point blank. The arsenal is filled with a vast amount of artillery of every size and every improvement, besides huge stacks of rifles and muskets, enough to "put the world in arms." Then the artillery wagons, and the baggage wagons, and the camp wagons, all filling an immense inclosure around the arsenal, give to the place really a very warlike appearance. The wagons are made strong, but light, and their bodies consist of willow-osier work. I really envied the Austrian government the having so many of these light and handsome wagons, for I think I could put a few of them to far better uses than hauling gunpowder and cannon balls. I would put them to hauling sugar-cane, and fill their ample sides with swelling ears of Indian corn. "Peace has its conquests as well as war." I much prefer to fight crab-grass and cockle-burs, to mortal men of flesh and blood; and such modest unpretending tools as the plough, the hoe, and the spade, are much more congenial to my nature than broadswords, smooth-bores, and grape-shot.

Last night I went to the opera, and was much delighted at the fine music. The theatre or opera house is not so fine as that at Berlin; the music is, however, delightful, perhaps the very best in the world.

To-day being Sunday, I have spent in visiting the churches. I heard mass at St. Peter's. The singing was good, and the organ well played. At the church of the Capuchins lie the mortal remains of all of the House of Hapsburg. Here also reposes Napoleon II., Duke of Reichstadt, by the side of his mother Maria Louisa. An arrangement is already made by which the body of the young Napoleon will soon be taken to Paris, and placed by the side of his illustrious sire. The finest cathedral in Vienna, however, is St. Stephen's. It was begun as early as 1359, and completed in 1433. The steeple is 428 feet high, and the largest bell, cast out of 180 Turkish cannon, weighs 40,000 pounds! In this church is buried the celebrated Prince Eugene, the great general and companion-in-arms of the Duke of Marlborough. In the church of St. Augustine is a magnificent monument to the memory of the Duchess Christiana, by Canova. It represents an open tomb, with several figures (in marble) as large as life, walking into it. It is a most beautiful conception, and well worthy of the great artist. In this same church, in the Loretto chapel, are all the hearts of the members of the Hapsburg family, preserved in silver urns.

In this great capital there are hundreds of elegant palaces. Among them Prince Lichtenstein's, Prince Esterhazy's, Count Czernin's, and Count Schönborn's, are the principal. In all these palaces are fine galleries of paintings and statuary, costly jewels, and rare articles of *virtu*. The imperial cabinets of antiquities and of minerals are the very best in existence. Here are the finest specimens of the various minerals that the earth and sea contain, and most tastefully arranged, with appropriate descriptions. Among them I noticed a pearl as large as my fist. It looked as if all the rays of the rainbow had been concentred in it. Here are precious stones of every description in the largest profusion, from Golconda's precious gems "of purest ray serene," to Ural's malachite, all "dressed in living green." Here is seen gold from "Afric's burning sands," and white granite from "Greenland's icy mountains."

To the student of nature, to the lover of the natural sciences, this imperial collection is a treat indeed. My companion, Dr. Smith, is a fine geologist, and naturally a great lover of its kindred science mineralogy. He lingered for hours and hours examining these fine specimens of nature's wealth; at last when compelled to leave, sighed to find that he could not stay longer. Around the city of Vienna are a great many places of amusement and attraction. The Prater is an immense inclosure, (the Hyde Park of Vienna,) and is well studded with fine shady trees, and interspersed with groups of shrubbery and nice resting-places for the million. Here are thousands of tame deer for the Imperial tables. In the suburbs, only a mile or two, is the palace of Schönbrun, the summer residence of the emperor. Napoleon lived here when he was master of Vienna, and here his son, the

Duke of Reichstadt, lived and died. The gardens attached to this palace are beautiful; they extend up the sides of the mountain on which is built "the Gloriette," a beautiful, airy, open summer-house, on the top of which is a promenade, commanding a most magnificent view of Vienna and its environs. Near this "Gloriette" is Hitteldorf, the emperor's grounds, inclosed by a high stone wall, and containing 3,000 wild boars; and here is the place where the Austrian aristocracy assemble every fall to amuse themselves in that time-honored German sport of " hunting the boar." With us matters are reversed; the *bores* hunt us, and generally succeed, much to our annoyance, in finding us!

I went this evening to hear the celebrated Straus, (pronounced Strows.) He plays with his band every Sunday evening at a fashionable establishment in the suburbs of Vienna. The music was truly magnificent, especially the waltzes and schottishes, for which Straus has so long been famous. There is a story here that Straus was once deep in love with a daughter of the archduke. His love was not appreciated or requited. On her wedding-day he was summoned to attend with his band, and play for the assembled guests, the bridal party. He did so, and composed expressly for the occasion a waltz which was played then, but has never been performed since. The blushing bride asked him to play one of his sweetest waltzes; immediately he obeyed. She took the floor with her partner. The music was splendid—on went the waltz—the music was delicious—still the waltz went on—the music became ravishing—the waltz went on and on and on—sweeter and sweeter was the music—faster and faster became the waltz, until the beautiful bride dropped dead upon the floor, a victim to the intoxicating influence of Straus's music! I do not know whether this story be true or not, but one thing I do know, that his waltzes are really charming; and if any thing in the shape of music could kill a man or a woman, Straus's waltzes would. I wish I could write you more about this great city, for to me it is the most agreeable and interesting of all the cities I have visited. The women here, notwithstanding the pouting Austrian lip, are beautiful, and exceedingly agreeable and kind to strangers. As a "looker on in Vienna," I have learned much in this imperial city, and shall always congratulate myself in having visited it. At present, the great drawback to Austrian prosperity is the wretched condition of her currency. This is 20 per cent. below par. She pays and feeds this day 600,000 soldiers! No wonder the nation is impoverished and the treasury bankrupt. Adieu,

     Yours truly,
         H. W. A.

LETTER NO. XXII.

Hotel de La Ville, Trieste, Austria.
Sept. 30, 1859.

Editors Advocate:

From Vienna to this place is 363 miles, time 24 hours, fare 34 florins, or $17. The railway passes over the Styrian Alps, or rather under them, for I counted 47 tunnels! Our roads across the Alleghanies and the Cumberland Mountains are works of great skill, but this is the most herculean enterprise I have ever seen. It is a double track the whole distance, and built in the most substantial manner. The scenery as you pass along through Styria is very fine, resembling in a very remarkable manner the most picturesque portions of Switzerland. I noticed that the farmers along the road in many places plant our Indian corn, and cut it while green as fodder for their horses and cattle. Indeed this seems to be their principal crop, and appears to have taken the place of the grasses in a great degree. Buckwheat also flourishes well here, and is generally grown. The zigzag course of the cars as they wind around the mountains, gives the traveller a beautiful panorama of the country through which he passes. One station is on the very top of a high peak of the Alps; you then descend gradually, and dive into the bowels of the earth for a mile or two, and come out within a few hundred yards from the place where you began the descent. As we approached the Adriatic, we could see the far-off Carpathian Mountains on the confines of Hungary. For miles and miles before you reach the Adriatic, the whole country is one wild, rugged, barren waste, with but a few scattering huts, and no evidences of civilization. This portion of Illyria is only occupied as sheep walks, for I did not see an inclosure of any kind, not even a garden spot. The whole country seems to be one huge, rugged, ill-shapen rock, covered with mosses and lichens which afford a scanty subsistence for sheep and goats. As the sun rose o'er this cold and bleak region, we came in sight of the calm and beautiful Gulf of Venice.

Trieste, the principal commercial city of Austria, (in fact the only seaport of any importance,) is situated at the head of the Adriatic or Gulf of Venice, and lies in the shape of a crescent. It contains about 80,000 inhabitants, most of whom are Italians, Greeks, and Turks. But few *white* people live here. I took a commissionaire and went over the place, but I must say was a good deal disappointed. There are no works of art here, no statuary, no paintings; commerce is king. This is the home of the celebrated Lloyd Steamers, which leave once a week for Constantinople, Alexandria, Smyrna, &c. Ships from all parts of the world are here, and on the quays are seen large quantities of cotton being reshipped to the various portions of the Austrian empire.

I went to-day to the celebrated Tergesteum, (a species of café,) and spent an hour in the conversation rooms. While I was sipping my coffee, a turbaned Turk as black as the ace of spades, with a shirt nearly as black as his skin, came up and took a seat by me on the large sofa, crossed his legs, and began puffing away his horrid tobacco smoke under my very nose. I felt like "taking by the throat the circumcised dog," and smiting him until he should know how to treat a Christian gentleman, but recollected that I was in Austria. Here soldiers march and counter-march. The roll of the drum is heard nearly every hour of the day. At every corner of the street you see a man with a long moustache and a gleaming bayonet. I saw in the market this morning fine figs and olives, peaches, apples, and melons, with any quantity of macaroni, raw, baked, fried, and stewed! Disgusting thing that macaroni! your real Turk eats it with his fingers.

On my way here from Vienna, I met with quite an adventure; I got into a row with the conductor. I had bought a through ticket; at the first station after leaving Vienna the conductor came along and asked for my ticket, (billet;) I gave it to him, and he passed on without clipping and returning it, as he should have done. At the next station he came along, and again asked for my ticket. I told him that he had it, and that it was a through ticket to Trieste. This he denied in a very emphatic manner. Here I of course was in a dilemma, quarrelling with an Austrian in very bad French! In the height and fury of our quarrel, a stranger sitting by me, a well-dressed and very intelligent Austrian, came to my relief. He could speak a little English and a little French, enough to make himself understood. We made the conductor count over his through tickets, and among them mine was found. The poor fellow made many apologies for his mistake, and during the route frequently took occasion to show me more than ordinary attention. My new acquaintance (the Austrian gentleman) on hearing that I was an American, asked a thousand questions about our country, and expressed a great desire to visit a land where the iron heel of despotism could not oppress the poor. He resided in the town of Gratz at the foot of the Alps, and left us on arriving at that place. He shook me warmly by the hand and said, "Mynheer, adieu, I wish you une bonne voyage—I loves Amerique. I shall see him yet before I die—may God mit his blessings go mit you and your grande Republique." This is the feeling everywhere in Europe in regard to our country, particularly among the middle and working classes. They all wish us God speed. Our only enemies, strange to say, are to be found at home, living under the same stars and stripes.

Since writing the above I have had dinner—beef-steak bad—pomme de terre worse—wine—Cyprus wine—oh Lord! it tastes more like squills or syrup of Ipecacuanha, than the juice of the grape. I drank a bottle of it—of course it made me sick. Took a sail-boat, and went a sailing on the Adriatic. Expected every moment to meet the Doge, but didn't do it. Passed a couple of Austrian regiments drilling on the plateau; they looked very fine soldiers, moved like clock-work. All did no good, however, at Magenta and Solferino: they have a plenty of bone and muscle, but lack the brain. Sailed down to Capo d'Istria, and saw the shores of Croatia; tacked about for the light-house in the Gulf of Trieste, and there, from the top of said light-house, saw the monarch of day sink to his rest in the bosom of the tranquil Adriatic—a glorious sight and one that I shall never forget.

Yours truly,
H. W. A.

LETTER NO. XXIII.

Hotel de l'Europe, Venice, Italy,
September 23, 1859.

Editors Advocate:

"I stood in Venice on the bridge of sighs,
A palace and a prison on each hand."

On yesterday morning, at sunrise, I arrived in this city of palaces, "that spring from the sea." The first human being I saw was an Austrian soldier. There are now in Venitia 260,000 Austrian soldiers, and all seem ready to have another fight for the honor of the House of Hapsburg. The Venetians are very much dissatisfied with the treaty of Villa Franca, and are daily giving Austria much trouble. Last night as I was walking along the Piazza di San Marco, I heard the report of two guns. I went in the direction whence the crowd was rushing, and found two Italians lying dead, weltering in their own blood. They had attempted to take the muskets from the Austrian soldiers, while they were on guard. It is generally believed that before spring the Austrian soldiers will enter Milan. All classes here are down on Napoleon for not freeing them from Austrian tyranny. It seems to be a national idea. Even the Lazzaroni, who live by begging and stealing, are long and loud in their curses of Napoleon.

Venice is a city *sui generis*. It has a population of 100,000 inhabitants. This is the only city in the world, I believe, in which there are no carriages or horses, cattle or asses. (Fortunate city that, in which there are no asses!) The city is divided by a grand canal, into which a thousand small canals lead, and is built on 72 islands. All the travel is done by gondolas. These are long, narrow boats, invariably painted black. They have movable covers, and generally carry four persons. As these dark-looking boats skim along the silent canals, they remind you more of hearses than any thing else. The gondolier is a hardy, dark-looking man, and handles his oar with great ease and dexterity. To while away the time, he generally sings some Italian sonnet, and thus makes your voyage very agreeable.

Venice is rich in churches and private palaces. There are 30 cathedrals here, all possessing great interest to the traveller. But the pride of Venice is San Marco. This is the most remarkable building in the world, for precious stones and rare marbles. The interior is literally one entire mosaic. There are no paintings in oil. The altar-piece is of solid gold, and thickly set with precious stones.

The front doors of the cathedral are of bronze, and were brought from Constantinople. On entering this church you are completely bewildered, in looking at the great profusion of porphyry, verde antique, alabaster, lapis lazuli, and every other kind and color of precious stones and marbles, from all parts of the world. When I first heard that beautiful song,

"I dreamed that I dwelt in marble halls,"

I never expected to have it in my power to realize the poet's idea. San Marco is now the noblest specimen the world has ever produced of "marble halls," for it is so rich and splendid, that upon beholding it, you would almost swear that Aladdin, with his powerful lamp, had been there. The square fronting the cathedral is called the Piazza di San Marco, and here are collected the fashion and *élite* of the city in the evening, to listen to the imperial band, to promenade, make love and drink coffee. I must confess that I do not think the Venetian ladies so "killing pretty." From Lord Byron, down to the lesser poets, all have gone quite crazy about the dark flowing tresses, large languishing eyes, and sylph-like forms of the Venetian ladies. I saw none of these angelic beings; those I saw were any thing but beautiful. They all look sad, sorrowful, and sulky; half-starved, yellow-skinned, and bony. I saw them by day and also by night, when they looked no better.

The gondoliers and beggars make up about one-half of the population of Venice. Wherever you go, on the street, in the palace, in the church, at the hotel, the eternal beggars are sure to find you.

There are many very fine private palaces here, all of which are thrown open to the public, and for a small sum to the porter, you can go through their elegant chambers and fine galleries of paintings. In one of them to-day I saw the chef d'œuvre of the great Conova, his Ajax and Hector. These palaces are filled with an immense number of fine paintings by the old masters, and some of the very best statuary in Italy. The rooms are cased with variegated marble, the floors with mosaics, and the ceilings covered with frescoes, making them the most elegant and luxurious chambers I ever saw. The Palazzo Grimian belongs to the Duchess de Berri, who spends her winters here, and gives most magnificent parties. Another palace belongs to the celebrated danseuse Taglioni, who also spends her winters here, and entertains handsomely. All of these palaces are splendid inside, and kept in very neat and elegant order, but show a dilapidated exterior. The marble has been eaten away by the "hungry tooth of time;" the walls are blackened and always damp, while seaweeds and barnacles cling to the very sills of the doors.

The residences of Mrs. Adams and of Messrs. Andrews and Randolph of Iberville, are far more showy and much more comfortable than any private palace in Vienna. The Rialto is a marble bridge across the Canalazzo, or grand canal, and has a span of 100 feet. It is very solid and compact, being entirely built of pure marble. This is the place where Shylock and Antonio met once upon a time, and here the merchants of Venice did " mostly congregate." But, alas! what a falling off is there. This bridge now, instead of being the popular resort for the wealthy merchants, is occupied by stalls for the sale of miserable cheap jewelry and children's toys. The principal trade, however, on the Rialto, seems to be in onions and mushrooms. Here in the very centre of the bridge, are stacks of onions; onions in baskets, onions on strings, onions in every conceivable shape and manner. The Venetian ladies are said to be very fond of this esculent, and labor under the happy belief that the aroma of the onion is a most delicious and delicate perfume.

The Palazzo Ducale is one of the most remarkable palaces in Venice. It adjoins the San Marco, and was for many years the residence of the doges. It is filled with many fine paintings, many of them of gigantic size. Underneath this palace are the state-prisons. From the Ducal Palace is a narrow way that leads to the " Bridge of Sighs," or as the Italians call it, Ponte di Sospiri. It is a high, covered, narrow stone bridge, that leads from the Hall of Justice to the prisons. The state prisoners were sent by a secret passage to the hall of justice. If condemned, they were sent across this fatal bridge to the dark, deep dungeons, " whence no unfortunate traveller ever returned." When I stood upon this Bridge of Sighs, I thought of the thousands of unhappy wretches who had trodden these cold stones, on their way to torture and to death. But the murderers and the murdered have long since appeared before a just and upright Judge; and many a cruel prince and wicked doge have been compelled to walk that eternal bridge of sighs, into far deeper and blacker dungeons than were ever seen in Venice.

I have spent this day pretty much in my gondola, and have threaded every hole and corner in this singular city. There are 4,000 gondolas in Venice. You hire them generally by the hour. The usual price per hour is 1 zwanziger, or 14 cents. Venice is certainly a very bad place for a drunken man, for the deep salt water (20 feet deep) comes up to the very door-sill of every house, the tide rising here only about 3 feet. The city reminds one of Cairo, (Illinois,) or Napoleon, (Arkansas,) or Lake Providence, (La.,) in time of a crevasse. If I were the father of a dozen or more children, I do not think I should settle in Venice, unless they were all web-footed.

Ever since I have been here I have involuntarily been on the look-out for old Shylock and Antonio, for the Moor and his Lieutenant Cassio, for Pierre and Priuli. Alas! they have all gone to their long homes. The gonfalons of Venice no longer wave from the Piazzo San Marco. Her winged lions crouch before the double eagle of her conqueror, while the very palace of the doges has become a common barrack for Austrian soldiers.

In going to the Café Florian to-day, I met a Shylock—a veritable Shylock. As he passed me with a bag of gold in his hand, he gave it a closer grip, and stared at me as if he could cut a pound of Christian flesh from next my heart, without even batting his eyes.

Venice is perhaps more remarkable for its beautiful Piazzo San Marco, than any thing else. It is a large oblong area, 562 feet long by 232 wide, and is surrounded by elegant buildings on every side. In the Piazza is a lofty square tower or campanile, 316 feet high and 42 feet square. From the top of this tower the prospect is truly delightful. On one side you see the mouths of the Adige and the Po, and on the other the placid waters of the beautiful Adriatic.

Venice has given the world some of the best painters. Here were born Titian and Tintoretto. This was the home of Paul Veronese, and the great Leonardo da Vinci.

Venice has but little commerce. Its revenues are all absorbed by the Austrian rulers, to support their immense standing army. Occasionally an American ship comes here, loaded with cotton or tobacco. But the principal revenue brought to the city is by strangers. Many English and Americans spend their winters here, and thus distribute a good deal of money.

Watches and jewelry of all kinds, particularly

a very delicate species of gold chain, are manufactured here in large quantities. But one thing I was surprised to see, or rather not to see. There is not a *Venetian blind* in all Venice!

To our very popular consul, Mr. Sarmiento, of Philadelphia, I am under many obligations. He showed me much attention, and contributed much to my enjoyment while in Venice.

Yours truly,
H. W. A.

LETTER NO. XXIV.

Hotel de la Rose, Milan, Italy,
Sept. 26, 1859.

Editors Advocate :

From Venice to Milan is 176 miles—fare by rail 32 liras, or about $5 50. I, however, did not go on directly to Milan, but stopped at Padua, Verona, and Solferino. Padua is an old, seedy place, with the grass growing in the middle of the streets. It has a few fine churches, and a university, which is still much patronized by Italian students. The public square or grand piazza is a very pretty place filled with statues. I noticed in one of the largest and finest churches of Padua, a large quantity of army stores—barrels of meal, and bread, and oats, all piled upon the beautiful tessellated marble floors! What a desecration! In this church is a painting by Paul Veronese, which would command almost any price in our country, but it hangs now on deserted walls, as the priest refuses to perform divine service in a church desecrated by a tyrannical soldiery. Padua is 23 miles by rail from Venice, and has a population of 50,000 inhabitants. It followed the fortunes of Venice, and is now a part of the Lombardo-Venetian kingdom. Its Palace of Justice contains an immense chamber, or hall, covered with many curious frescoes. I noticed in Giotto's chapel a most remarkable piece of art; it is by the sculptor Agostino Fasolata, and is called "Lucifer and his companions cast out from Heaven." It is composed of 60 figures, all carved out of one block of Carrara marble. The Café Peddrochi is the finest building of the kind in Italy, and kept in a very elegant manner. After spending the day in Padua, I got a most excellent dinner at the Hotel de la Stella d'Or, and set out late in the evening for Verona.

From Padua to Verona is 50 miles. Already the atmosphere told me that I was among the mountains, for the night became cool and pleasant. After a delightful night's rest, I took breakfast on melons and fruits, and began my daily labors.

Verona is situated near the gorges of the Tyrol, and is surrounded by the fortresses of Peschiera, Mantua, and Legnago. It is inclosed by a series of turreted walls, and the cannon frown down upon you in every direction from rampart, bastion, and parapet. The Adige, a bold and muddy stream, divides Verona into almost equal parts. It is a rapid river, that rushes down from the Tyrolese Alps, and furnishes great water power to the manufacturers of silks, and woollens, and cottons. The current is so rapid that the mills are all turned by breast-wheels simply placed in the water, and the machinery attached thereto.

Verona has a population of 48,000 inhabitants, and contains the most perfect ancient amphitheatre in existence. It is in a perfect state of repair, and is almost nightly used as a theatre. It is 1,533 feet in circumference, and 100 feet high, and is filled with a regular succession of stone steps or seats. This immense amphitheatre will comfortably seat 30,000 persons at a time! Here it was that gladiators fought to amuse the assembled mob of noble Romans, and it was here that many a primitive Christian was torn to pieces by wild beasts.

Shakspeare has located two of his best plays in Verona—the two Gentlemen of Verona, and Romeo and Juliet. The tomb of Juliet is yet seen in the garden of the Orfanotrofio. It is of red Verona marble, and is much injured by visitors, who not only scratch their names all over it, but break off pieces and carry them away. Poor Juliet, she had a hard time of it—for death, not Romeo, came and took her maiden *heart*. Verona is said to be rich in ancient curiosities and literature. Here are the tombs of the Scaligers, a curious monument of the middle ages. It is remarkable for its dye-works and silk manufactures, in which departments the Veronese excel all other Italians. Many distinguished men were born here, among them Cornelius Nepos, Catullus, the elder Pliny, Paul Veronese, and the Marquis Maffei.

From Verona to what they now call the frontier is a short distance, only 8 miles. Here is Peschiera, where the Mincio leaves the Lago di Garda, and is now the terminus of Austrian territory. Between this place and the next Italian town, Desenzano, was fought the great battle of Solferino. I stopped here two hours and examined the localities. It is the nicest place in the world for a fight, as our friend Sir Lucius O'Trigger would say. The village of Solferino is off the road about six miles, and is situated on a hill. Here the Austrians were intrenched, with their lines extending across the railroad. The whole country around is a level plain, and is one large mulberry orchard. In order to obstruct the French cavalry as much as possible, the Austrians cut down all the mulberry trees for miles, and dug ditches in every direction, but all this did no good; the Zouaves and Turcos leaped ditches, mulberry trees, and every thing else, and bayoneted the Austrians at their very guns. At present there is but little or no sign of the great and bloody battle, except the numerous fresh-made graves. In one trench alone lie the bodies of 800 soldiers, and there they will lie, till Gabriel shall sound a far louder blast than ever was heard on the dreadful field of Solferino.

Within a few yards of each other are stationed the Austrian and Sardinian sentries, for this whole country is yet a military camp. Just as soon as you cross the Sardinian line, you see the difference. In Austrian Italy all is silent, dark, and dreary. You seldom, if ever, hear any conversation in the cars; and when a man speaks, he always looks around to see who is present. But in Sardinia, every man and woman is discussing freely Italian politics. There is mirth and laughter, and even song, while everybody is hurrahing for Victor Emanuel. While in the cars, I witnessed a very animated and rather acrimonious discussion between a lady from Milan and a gentleman from Venice. The subject was Garibaldi. The lady seemed devoted to him, and praised him above all others; declared him to be her beau ideal of a hero and a brave man. The gentleman, by the way a very well-dressed, intelligent person, denounced him as a pitiful upstart—a miserable, robbing, fillibustering scoundrel, who had no home, but like an Arab was wandering about, and selling himself to fight where there was no chance of being killed. Both parties became very much excited, and I looked every moment to see the lady draw her stiletto, and stab the traducer of Garibaldi to the heart, for I find that he is almost idolized here. Besides, the women of Italy are passionate; and all carry a nice little stiletto, a perfect love of a thing, secreted in the ample folds of their dresses. No blood, however, was shed, for we were now arrived at Milan, and all hastened to the hotel, it being late at night.

Milan is an immense city. It has nearly 200,000 inhabitants, and for ages has been the capital of Lombardy, and the centre of the fashion, and intelligence, and wealth of Northern Italy. The climate here is much colder, and the people appear almost a different race of beings from the Venetians. They are fine, stout, good-looking men, who stood up at Solferino like clever fellows, and gave the Austrians the very d—l. Milan is at present entertaining the six deputies who came to see Victor Emanuel from the states of the Romagna. Last night the city was beautifully illuminated, and the deputies made speeches from the balconies of the La Scala to the people. Every thing went off finely. Although there was a very large gathering, still there was no disturbance of any kind, or even unpleasant accident to mar the pleasures of the evening. The people of Lombardy sympathize very much with their brethren of Bologna and Ferrara, and the rest of the Papal states, and are determined to free them from their present tyranny.

There are many fine works of art here, in painting and statuary. The modern living artists appear to excel, and are well patronized. In the Brera (the Gallery of Arts) I found a large number of very fine paintings, mostly however by living artists, who are to be seen here daily at work amid the throng of strangers who are crowding Milan at present. In the Refectory of the church of Santa Maria delle Grazie is the world-renowned painting of "The Last Supper," by Leonardo da Vinci. Although much injured by time, and more by the damp walls, still it is a magnificent work of genius, from which copies are being taken continually. The original painting is a fresco, and covers the whole of one end of the Refectory.

Yesterday was Sunday. I went to hear mass at the Duomo, the great cathedral, second only to St. Peter's at Rome. It is 500 feet long, 350 feet high, and 275 feet wide, all built of solid white marble, a most astonishing work of architectural art. The roof is supported by 60 immense pillars of marble, twelve feet in diameter. The entire cathedral is literally covered with statuary. It was illuminated last night, and as I came in from Lake Como, the cupola looked like an immense ball of fire suspended in the air.

I took rail yesterday, and went out to Lake Como —one hour's ride—and there spent the day, having taken a steamer that makes the usual tour of the lake daily, returning to the town of Como in the evening, in time for the cars to Milan. This is a lovely lake: Bulwer, in his "Lady of Lyons," has not overdrawn the picture. Nature has been lavish in her works here, and what she has failed to do, art has supplied. The shores of Como do not possess the rich cultivation of Zurich, nor the wild grandeur of Lucerne; the water is not so blue as Leman, nor so deep and secluded as Loch Lomond, but the hundreds of beautiful villas and elegant palaces that spring from the very water's edge, the numerous fountains and fairy grottoes, the rich green of the olive and the mulberry, and above all, the delightful climate, and calm, smooth surface of the water, "glassing softest skies," makes Lake Como the most lovely spot on earth.

The principal manufacture of Milan is silk. This is the great central depot for the silk market of Italy. For miles around the city, in fact, through the whole of Northern Italy, the mulberry abounds and is the main growth, on the leaves of which the silkworm is fed. There is a great deal of style here. The streets are well paved, and the equipages gotten up with great taste. While here, I have visited the Opera, La Scala. It is the largest Opera House in the world, and can comfortably seat 6,000 persons. The opera given was Cleopatra; the ballet was magnificent. There were 500 ballet girls at one time on the stage, and such a standing on big toes, and sailing of "dry goods," and *pirouetting* around generally, was never seen before. The dancers are young and pretty, and dress with great taste. Only imagine 500 beautiful fairy forms before you, cutting up all sorts of *didos*. It is enough to run a man perfectly crazy, and make him wish that he were another Briareus, with a hundred arms, to hug them all at once. I began this letter at Lake Como, and am now finishing it on the battle-field of Magenta. I shall mail it at Turin, and sleep to-morrow night at Genoa. Adieu,

Very truly yours,
H. W. A

LETTER NO. XXV.

Genoa, Italy, *Oct.* 1, 1859.

Editors Advocate:

Since I wrote you last I have visited Turin, Alessandria, and Genoa. I found Turin quite a city, and most beautifully situated in a valley between high mountains. It has a population of 125,000 inhabitants, and is the capital of Piedmont, and of the now great kingdom of Sardinia. Victor Emanuel resides here in great state, and seems to govern a prosperous and happy people. Of all the crowned heads of Europe, he and Napoleon are the only ones who have smelt " the villanous saltpetre," on the battle-field. The Sardinian king looks every inch a soldier, and is evidently no carpet knight.

The Royal Palace is a very fine building, elegantly furnished with all sorts of royal finery. In it are many fine paintings. In this palace is a full suite of rooms, now unoccupied, belonging to the sister of the king. She had married " a right royal husband," in the person of a distinguished prince, and was most elegantly domiciliated in the palace. A few years ago her husband died, and the disconsolate widow married an humble colonel. Court etiquette could not brook this misalliance, and now, on the banks of Lake Como, the widow and the colonel are as happy as two turtle-doves.

Turin has a most delightful climate. It lies between the Alps and Apennines, on the banks of the Po. This river here is quite small at present, but rises to a great and fearful height in the spring, when the snows melt. Even here large levees have to be erected, to keep in the "swelling flood," and when they break a vast country overflows, carrying death and destruction through the land.

The fruits here are very fine. The grapes and figs are sweeter than in any part of Italy. At the hotels they give you bread baked in a very singular shape. Imagine a handful of pipe-stems about 18 inches long, baked brown, and placed by the side of your plate, and you can form some idea of the fashion of baking bread in Turin. The place has the air of a capital city; is the centre of the military and civil power of the kingdom, and is blessed with beautiful fountains and wide streets. The second stories of all the houses project over the street, in such a manner as to make delightful walks and promenades, even in bad weather. I have seen only one other city in my travels, where these comfortable sidewalks are so well arranged, and that is Berne, the capital of Switzerland.

The inhabitants of Turin are principally engaged in the manufacture of silks. The surrounding country produces rice and Indian corn in large quantities.

Victor Emanuel seems to be very popular here with all classes, and has in a large degree the affections of his people. For several years a strange quarrel has been going on between him and the pope. The court of Sardinia, at the suggestion of Count Cavour, the prime minister, has sold a very large property belonging to the church and the monasteries, and placed the proceeds in the treasury of the state. The church, of course, protested, and the pope was appealed to. The Holy Father ordered the sales to be cancelled and the property restored, but unfortunately Victor Emanuel is king in his own realm, and sets the decrees of the pope at defiance. It is said that a bull will soon be issued from " Imperial Rome."

The political excitement here is very great. Count Cavour has resigned, and retired to the country to live, for he boldly says that Piedmont is now nothing but a dependence to France. The Zouaves are still in Milan in large numbers, while the streets of Genoa are filled with soldiers. From one end of Piedmont to the other drums are beating, bayonets are gleaming, and all seems ready for another conflict.

From Turin to Genoa you go by railway; distance 103 miles; fare 16 francs. On the route the most remarkable places are " the battle-field of

Marengo," and the fortress of Alessandria. This celebrated battle-field lies close to the village of Marengo, and is seen from the railroad. The village is insignificant in itself, but has given the name to one of "the bloodiest pictures in the book of time." It is an elevated plain on the banks of the Tanaro, and not far from Alessandria, where the Bormida joins the Tanaro, making quite a stream. Alessandria has for ages been a fortress that is deemed impregnable. It is considered the key to the whole of this country, and is kept in good repair and well garrisoned. It was to this place that poor old Melas, the Austrian general, rode in great haste to inform the authorities that he had gained the victory at Marengo. But most unfortunately for him, Desaix came up and rallied the French soldiers, when upon a second charge the tables were turned; the Austrians were vanquished, and poor old Melas had to sue for peace, and take such terms as Napoleon saw proper to give.

The country around here looks unhealthy. It is all subject to overflow, and breeds terrible fevers. Before reaching Genoa the face of the country, for many miles, assumes a rugged and broken appearance. The cork-tree here assumes its amplest proportions, and presents its bare and naked trunk to the curious gaze of every passer-by. This corktree is a species of glandiferous quercus, and resembles in a great degree our live-oak. It is an evergreen, and grows to a large size. Our patent office has distributed large quantities of acorns through the country, and I do hope the tree may flourish in our land, as it would be very desirable to plant such a tree in our villages and court-yards, where everybody has an indefeasible right to tie everybody's horse to a shade-tree, and let everybody's aforesaid horse bite, destroy, and completely eat up the aforesaid shade-trees. Now the cork-tree will be the very thing, for the more you bite it the better it grows. It likes to be bit. You could not please it better.

Genoa is a great city. It has improved very much since the days of Christopher Columbus, and now rivals Marseilles. It has a population of 150,000 inhabitants. The principal capital seems to be invested in shipping, for this is a great seaport. There are also large manufactories here of silks and velvets; of gold and silver filagree work; of all kinds of jewelry, and quite an extensive trade carried on in paintings and statuary.

The ladies of Genoa dress very beautifully; they all wear a long white veil thrown over their heads, which gives them a fairy-like appearance. I did not see a bonnet in all Genoa. The streets are very narrow; in many parts of the city the smallest carriage cannot pass. Every thing is packed on mules. The city is called "Genoa Superba," on account of its numerous marble palaces. The two finest streets, the Nuovo and the Nuovissimo, are indeed magnificent specimens of Italian grandeur. The city is situated very much like Vicksburg, Mississippi, and is a good deal "up and down." I visited many of the private palaces, and found in them an immense number of paintings, but none of them very remarkable. The universal stone here is marble; marble palaces and marble cottages; marble churches and marble stables!

The cathedrals and churches are among the most gorgeous in Europe. The St. Lorenzo is a magnificent pile, with columns in front taken at the capture of Almeria, and transported to this cathedral, as part of the spoils. The richest portion of the church is the chapel of St. John the Baptist, into which no female is permitted to enter, an exclusion imposed by Pope Innocent VIII. The Palazzo Rossi blazes with every thing that elegant taste could suggest or money buy. It is one mass of fine paintings, rare statuary, and gold and silver vessels of every kind.

The fruits here are delightful. All kinds in the greatest profusion; oranges and bananas, figs and grapes, peaches and pears.

Asses, huge leather-lunged fellows, are seen and heard at every corner of the street, while the muleteer, with his long whip, is driving his mules, single file, along the narrow streets.

The harbor is a most excellent one, and is filled with shipping from all parts of the world. I thought to myself, if old Christopher could only rise from his tomb some bright morning, and see our ship of war, the Wabash, (that now guards the

Mediterranean,) come into port, what would he say! I think, after examining the noble ship for a while, he would ask to have one broadside fired, and then, amid the smoke "of ignited sulphur," he would take his departure, with feelings of unspeakable pleasure and pride, that his own Western Continent had sent to the old world such a noble specimen of naval architecture, manned by such a crew of gallant seamen.

Adieu. I shall write you from Pisa.

Yours truly,
H. W. A.

LETTER NO. XXVI.

Pisa, Italy, *Oct.* 3, 1859.

Editors Advocate:

I arrived at Leghorn yesterday morning, after a very disagreeable night at sea. As we left Genoa a storm came on, the thunders rolled, the lightnings flashed, and the winds blew. I wished myself back on land again, a thousand times, I assure you, for I became very sea-sick. At 7 o'clock in the morning we reached Leghorn, where a new trouble was awaiting me. It appears that there was some informality in my passport, and I, together with another American, was detained on board the ship, and forbidden to land. I wrote to the American consul, who immediately sent me a permit from the local police, and I was permitted, after much trouble, to land in the one-horse city of Leghorn. The American whom I have just alluded to, was a citizen of New York, so said his passport, signed by Lewis Cass, Secretary of State; but strange to say, he could not speak one word of English! He, it seems, was a native of Florence, and had fled many years ago, "for his country's good." Now the revolution had taken place—the Grand Duke had fled—the whole country had declared for Victor Emanuel, and he thought it a good opportunity to visit again his old home, and the friends of his youth. On his arrival in Leghorn he was met by many an old acquaintance, and such a shaking of hands and kissing (French fashion) I never did see.

Leghorn is quite a city, having considerable manufactures in the way of straw hats and bonnets, silk and cotton goods. Here is also carried on quite a trade in amber, coral, mosaics, and cigars —the best cigars I have seen in Europe, for this is what is called a free port. It is the seaport for Tuscany and the Papal States, and thus enjoys quite a fair business in the shipping line. The shops here are well filled with Turkish articles of merchandise, and all sorts of marble and alabaster carvings. There is a marble group here on the quay, representing Cosimo surrounded by four black Turks kneeling and in chains, taken by him at the great battle of Lepanto. The group is by John of Bologna, and is an astonishing piece of sculpture, and attracts much attention.

Leghorn has a population of 80,000 inhabitants. It has but few or no evidences of antiquity; all the houses, streets, and monuments being of modern date. Here the *élite* of Tuscany assemble during the summer months to enjoy the fine seabathing, and thus give it the air of a fashionable city. In this city are 12,000 Jews; they have a magnificent synagogue, said to be the finest in the world.

From Leghorn to Pisa is only 12 miles. In company with a very intelligent silk merchant of Lyons, I left for Pisa; the road passes up the valley of the Arno, through a low, marshy country, which seems to be used only as pasture land. Cattle thrive well on these grounds: we passed immense herds of huge white bullocks, that seemed very fat.

Poor old Pisa! full of fleas and beggars. It has no commerce—no trade of any kind. The grass grows rank in all its streets, even up to the very door of her greatest curiosity, the "Leaning Tower." There is a population here of about 20,000 inhabitants, who seem to live, like some of the first families of Virginia, on *past recollections*. Pisa is rich in that species of wealth. The poet Dante often alludes to Pisa in his Inferno, and has told the sad story of Count Ugolino and his unhappy sons, in language that will never die.

The Duomo, (cathedral,) the Baptistery, the Campo Santo, (cemetery), and the Campanile, (Leaning Tower), are as interesting a group of buildings as any four edifices in the world. They group well together, and are seen to much advantage. They sometimes have quite an oriental appearance, when the large herd of camels belonging to the state, are seen feeding on the tall rich grass, in the shadow of these remarkable buildings.

The Duomo is one of the most remarkable monuments of the Middle Ages. It is 310 feet long, 230 wide, and is filled with the usual profusion of marble columns, mosaic pictures, tessellated floors, and silver altar-pieces. In it are a great many fine paintings, which are much prized for their great antiquity. One of these paintings is particularly beautiful, and possesses the very highest degree of true genius. It is the St. Agnes, by Andrea del Sarto. The Campo Santo is the ancient and classic burial-ground of Pisa and its surroundings. It was founded by Archbishop Ubaldo, in the year 1200. This prelate was expelled by Saladin from Palestine, and returned with 53 ships, loaded with earth taken from Mount Calvary. This sacred earth was said to reduce to dust, within 24 hours, all dead bodies buried in it. The Archbishop deposited this precious cargo in ground which he purchased in Pisa, and the present edifice was afterwards erected over it. It is an immense long building, 415 feet by 137, and contains a large collection of sepulchral monuments.

But the Campanile, or Leaning Tower, is the greatest curiosity of Pisa. Every schoolboy has seen a picture of it in his geography, and has often wondered why it did not fall down. It is, indeed, a remarkable structure. The tower is round; 53 feet in diameter, and 179 feet high. It is built of marble, and leans $13\frac{1}{2}$ feet out of perpendicular. You ascend it very easily, by a winding staircase of 294 steps. In going up, you feel very sensibly the *leaning side*, and imagine that you are about to fall. It is, however, as firm as the rock of ages, having now stood for nearly 700 years, having been built in A. D. 1174. As I passed into the tower, I noticed two lazzaroni playing cards under the steps. It reminded me so much of West Baton Rouge, and was an evidence of civilization that I never dreamed of in poor old decayed Pisa! In the Accademia delle Belle Arti, I noticed a splendid group of statuary by a living artist, Themistocles Guerrazzi. It represents the Exile with his wife and child, just in the act of landing on foreign soil. The exile is raising one foot from a rock marked "Italia," and has put down the other foot on a rock marked "America." The husband stands in a bold and manly position. His face is turned to Heaven, which he thanks, while sadness seems to oppress his soul in leaving his native land. While looking at this group of statuary, an aged Italian standing by me said, "I take you, sir, to be an American." "Yes," I replied, "I am." With tears in his eyes, and in a tremulous voice, he exclaimed, "I would to God that Italia was as free and as happy as America." Yes, thank God, we have a free and happy country, and long may we have stout hearts and strong arms to defend it.

The Baptistery is a circular building of marble, 99 feet in diameter, and 179 feet high. It is, as its name imports, simply built for baptizing, and is erected close to the cathedral. The walls are *eight feet* thick. This is the great secret of the durability of these old buildings. This is a building that has stood for nearly 600 years, for on one of the columns is the following inscription, " A. D. 1278. Edificata fuit de novo." The Baptistery possesses the echo principle in a most remarkable degree, and the Italians assemble here to sing for visitors, in order that they may listen to its magic powers. The notes of the human voice are here echoed four several and distinct times, and at last die away in the sweetest strains imaginable.

Adieu—I leave this evening for the loveliest spot on earth—that is, Florence—and shall write you what I think of it.

Very truly yours,
H. W. A.

LETTER NO. XXVII.

Hotel de l'Europe, Florence, Italy,
Oct. 5, 1859.

Editors Advocate:

I reached this delightful city day before yesterday, and am perfectly charmed with it. It has a population of 120,000 inhabitants, and is most beautifully situated in a valley of the Appenines. The Arno passes through it, and is spanned by four elegant bridges, ornamented with statuary. This celebrated river is a small stream, just 100 yards wide, and at present is very muddy, else I should be tempted to bathe in its classic waters.

My first act after arriving here was to call on our American sculptor, Hiram Powers. I found him in his studio, with apron and paper cap on, hard at work. He received me very kindly, and asked many questions about Louisiana, and particularly about *his Washington;* and when I told him how we all appreciated *his labor of love,* he seemed to feel it very much, and expressed his deep sense

of gratitude to Louisianians. He has just finished
"a California," an ideal piece. It is of Sienna
marble, much purer and better than Carrara. I
have never seen any thing to equal this statue.
His Greek Slave is very good, but does not equal
this. California is here represented as a full-grown,
beautiful woman, in a nude state. She displays all
her charms, inviting the whole world to come, but
holds a bunch of thorns concealed in her hand behind. Powers has lived here for 22 years. He is
a Vermonter by birth, and married a Philadelphia
lady. They have six children, two of them very
nice young ladies, highly accomplished in music,
and well educated. But one of his children (his
oldest son) has ever visited America. He came
over last year, and made some very fortunate in-
vestments in Kansas. I took tea and spent this
evening with his interesting family, and was highly
entertained. While at tea, Mr. Hart, from Ken-
tucky, another artist, came in, and we spent a delightful evening. Mr. Hart has just finished a colossal statue of Henry Clay, for Virginia, and is
now engaged on a bronze one of the same great
man, for New Orleans, to be placed on Canal street.
But to return to Powers. He is about 50 years
old, a very plain-looking, sensible man, with a remarkably fine gray eye, and an intelligent face.
Well may America be proud of Hiram Powers, for
he now ranks among the first of living sculptors.
His recent inventions of the sculptor's file; his
new application of power to the punch, and the

best uniform method of tempering steel, will alone render him a benefactor to the world. He is now engaged on a bust of Calhoun, having just finished America and Proserpine.

Florence has long been the home of modern arts and sciences. During the reign of the Medici family, and particularly the magnificent Lorenzo, Florence became the Athens of Europe. Even now it is what Rome was in the days of the Cæsars. Thousands of students flock here from all portions of the world, to study the art of painting and sculpture from the works of the grand old masters, only to be found in the Pitti and Uffizzi galleries. Here you see Raphael and Andrea del Sarto, Correggio and Carlo Dolce, Paulo Veronese and Titian, Sassoferato and Leonardo da Vinci, in all their glory. Here are Guido Reni and the divine Domenichino, Annibale Caracci and Fra Bartolomeo, Albani and Allori, all, all Italian artists of the very highest order.

The Pitti Palace is the residence of the grand duke. It is a huge structure, built of hammered stone; very plain and substantial to look at. In fact, as you approach it, it reminds you more of a fortress than a palace. The interior, however, is fitted up in the most gorgeous manner, and with oriental luxury. In the fourth story of this immense palace is the gallery of art. It is filled with the finest specimens of painting and statuary. The gallery is open every day from 10 to 3, except Sundays. No fee is required. The rooms are not only comfortable, but are fitted up magnificently with chairs and ottomans, and well heated in winter. Each room contains several hand catalogues in Italian and French. The floors are all of tessellated marble, and the ceilings are covered with appropriate frescos. These splendid apartments, about 50 in number, are all named after the classics. 1st, Hall of Venus. 2d, Hall of Apollo. 3d, Hall of Mars, etc., etc. In the Hall of Apollo are "The Hospitality of St. Julian," by Christoforo Allori; "Virgin and Child," by Murillo, and "The Deposition from the Cross," by Andrea del Sarto. In the Hall of Mars are the "Madonna della Seggiola," by Raphael, the sweetest of all his Madonnas; "Judith with the Head of Holofernes," a great master-piece of coloring, by Christoforo Allori; and "Rebecca at the Well," by Guido. In the Hall of Saturn are "The Descent from the Cross," by Perugino, and the "Vision of Ezekiel," by Raphael. These are only a few of the 500 paintings to be seen in this gallery. Besides are many apartments filled with antique statuary and Etruscan vases. Here also in this palace is seen that celebrated table, exhibited at the World's Fair in Paris, made of mother of pearl, lapis lazuli, jasper, agate, and chalcedony. This table is a great curiosity, and is a wonderful piece of mechanism. It is valued at $40,000.

Most of the flowers known to Botany are here represented, and in their true colors, as large as life; all without any artificial coloring. The varied tints and shading are made by a judicious adaptation of the gradations, which the materials afford. This is called Florentine mosaic, and is altogether different from the modern Roman mosaic. In the Roman mosaic the colors are artificial, they being formed of little pieces of opaque glass, called "smalto." In the Florentine, no colors are employed, except what are natural to the stone. By means of these only, the graceful and elaborate representations of flowers, fruit, birds, ornaments, butterflies, etc., have been produced. Marbles and jaspers, of brilliant colors, being of course very valuable, are only used in thin slices, like veneer one-eighth of an inch thick. The pattern is drawn on paper; each piece is then cut out and drawn on the stone chosen. The mosaic establishment here belongs to the government. Many hands are kept constantly employed. The process is so slow, and the details so tedious, that it takes months, and sometimes years, to make an ordinary-sized table.

From the Pitti Palace I went into the Boboli Gardens attached to the palace. These gardens are very extensive, and rise in terraces from the palace to the back walls. They are laid out with great taste, and are kept in most excellent order. The long living walls of laurel and cypress are relieved at almost every step by the most beautiful statuary. The climate here being very mild, the orange and citron, the olive and oleander, flourish well. These delightful gardens are much resorted to by all classes—the poor as well as the rich, who pass much of their time here, 'midst the fountains and flowers, the shaded walks and romantic grottoes of this earthly paradise.

After leaving the Boboli Gardens, I crossed the Arno, and wended my way to the Gallery of the Uffizi, called the "Imperial Galleria e Reale." It is the proudest boast of Florence, and has no equal in the wide world. The Uffizi is a large building, erected by order of Cosimo I., for the public offices and tribunals, and which, besides, contains the public library and the Medicean archives. This splendid gallery is arranged in a similar manner to the Pitti Palace, with beautiful apartments, all named. The most remarkable is the Tribune, in which are five of the best antique statues now in existence, to wit: the Venus de Medici, the Apollino, the Dancing Faun, the Wrestlers, and the Slave Whetting his Knife. The Venus de Medici is of course the most remarkable. It stands as the best representation of the female form. I must confess I did not like it. My impression is that the artists permit their veneration for the works of the ancients to warp their better judgments. In the first place, the head of the Venus is entirely too small, and the toes are too short. The arms placed in a very ungraceful position, and the whole figure has rather a " drooping, sheepish look." The lady is entirely naked, and of course should be *somewhat* ashamed. She, however, expresses in her countenance that "mauvaisse honte," which is never agreeable to the beholder. To my uneducated taste, the

Ariadne of Dannecker, at Frankfort, and the statuary at Charlottenburg, by Rauch, are far superior in every respect. But we will pass on to the paintings in this same room, the Tribune. On of the most remarkable is the "Virgin presenting the Infant to St. Joseph," by Michael Angelo; then comes Raphael in all his divine genius—his Madonna, (the Goldfinch,) then his "La Fornarina." This is the most exquisitely beautiful thing on canvas. It is a portrait of his own mistress. It is no angelic face, no *spirituelle* conception of ideal fancy, but a sure enough beautiful woman, of blood and flesh, capable of loving and being loved, and of continuing to love with passionate devotion, even beyond the grave. Here also is "St. John Preaching in the Desert," by Raphael. It looks as if it stood out from the canvas, and was ready to speak to you as you passed by.

Among the many glorious pictures in this magnificent gallery, are "The Venus," by Titian; "Adoration of the Magi," by Albert Durer; "The Virgin kneeling before the Infant Saviour," by Correggio; "Charles V.," by Vandyck; "Medusa's Head," by Leonardo da Vinci; "The Marriage at Cana," by Tintoretto; "Esther and Ahasuerus," by Paul Veronese; "Martyrdom of St. Sebastian," by Sodoma. A mere description of these treasures in the way of paintings, would fill a volume. This gallery contains 1,500 paintings, each of which would be considered a great prize in this country. Attached to the gallery is a room devoted to gems, and here are seen many antique cameos, with imperial portraits carved on them. Vespasian, Tiberius and Livia, Augustus and Galba, have all left their profiles on imperishable cameos, and done, as our friends the ancients did every thing, in true artistic style.

In leaving the pictures, you enter the gallery containing the statuary. Here are miles of "monumental marble," cut into every conceivable size and shape. First, is the Hall of Niobe, in which stand the statues of this unfortunate old lady, with her baker's dozen of sons and daughters, all shot and being shot at by the unerring arrows of the ruthless Apollo. As you pass along the immense corridor, you get into a perfect wilderness of antiques, man and beast, all confusedly mixed together.

'Twas late in the evening when I quit this immense gallery. My brain was completely bewildered with sight-seeing. I got all confused. The "Ancient Chimera" was jumbled up with the "Head of Holofernes;" while "the Dancing Faun" was pitching into "the Venus de Medici." I went to my hotel, and there I found our countryman Hiram Powers, who had just arrived to dine with me. We had an elegant dinner, and over a couple of bottles of best Italian wine, we discussed art and science, paintings and statuary, the Grand Duke and Victor Emanuel, not forgetting our own native land.

Adieu. I shall write you again from this place.
Yours truly,
H. W. A.

LETTER NO. XXVIII.

FLORENCE, ITALY, *Oct.* 8, 1859.

EDITORS ADVOCATE:

I wrote you a day or two ago from this city, since which time I have visited the churches and other public buildings, together with an occasional ride to the country. The Duomo or great cathedral is, of course, the most remarkable building in all Florence. It is called Santa Maria del Fiore. This is a monster building, and one of the very finest in Europe. It measures 500 feet in length, 306 in width, and 387 feet high. The dome is a wonderful triumph of human ingenuity. In grandeur and simplicity of construction, it is far superior to the domes of St. Mark at Venice, and of the cathedral of Pisa. It served as a model for Michael Angelo, in building the dome of St. Peter's at Rome. It is, in fact, the largest dome in the world, being $138\frac{1}{2}$ feet in diameter, and from the cornice of the drum to the eye of the dome, it is $133\frac{1}{4}$ feet. The architect was Brunelleschi, and his name is handed down with that of Michael Angelo, as one of the greatest architects that has ever lived. This stupendous cathedral is ornamented with a great deal of fine statuary on the outside. The interior is rather dark, owing to the smallness of the windows, the rich colors of the stained glass, and the sombre color of the stone with which it is built. Immense arches strengthen the pillars which support the huge dome; on these arches are sculptured the armorial bearings of Florence, of the Pope, of the Guelphs and the Ghibellines. The whole design is characterized by grandeur and simplicity. The pavement, being of various colored marbles, adds much to the magnificence and beauty of the structure. As you enter the cathedral, near the door is the portrait of Dante; on your left are Hell and Purgatory, painted in fresco; and in the centre, Paradise in small groups. Near the picture of Dante is a marble tomb ornamented with a cross between two shields, bearing eagles. It is the tomb of Conrad, the son and rival of the Emperor Henry IV.

Like Pisa, Florence has her Campanile or tower, and Baptistery. This tower is a beautiful specimen of Italian-Gothic architecture, and was intended by its builders to surpass any thing of the kind ever built by the Greeks or Romans, in their palmiest days of pride and power. It is a square structure, about the size of the Washington Monument at Washington City, and is $275\frac{3}{4}$ feet high. It is built of pure marble, and on the basement story are many sculptured reliefs from the Old and New

Testaments, the heathen mythology, the arts and sciences, music, poetry, philosophy, &c., &c. In one of these reliefs I noticed that the Deity is represented as pulling Eve bodily out of Adam's side, while he is asleep! On the west side, are the full-sized statues of the four Evangelists; one of them is called the "Zuccone," and it was to this statue the artist Donatello spoke, after he had given the last finishing stroke with the chisel. So pleased was he with his beautiful work, that he struck it, and exclaimed " Parla "—speak. You ascend this tower by a staircase of 414 steps, and when you reach the top, you are richly paid for your labor. Here the whole of Florence, with its beautiful environs, is laid out before you like a map. The Appenines on either hand, with their gentle slopes covered with the olive tree, now in full fruit. The Arno, like a silver thread, winding its devious course way off to the sea; while the wooded hills of Vallambrosa are seen far to the south-east. This prospect is truly delightful; it is one more of beauty than of grandeur, and far excels any other scene of this kind in the world. There is no city like Florence.

The Baptistery is in the form of an octagon, and supports a cupola and lantern. It is built of alternate layers of black and white marble, which give it a species of " half-mourning " appearance. Within, are 16 splendid antique columns of gray granite. At each side of the eastern gate is a dark and shattered shaft of porphyry, taken by the

Florentines at the conquest of Majorca, A. D. 1117. But the great ornaments to the Baptistery are the three bronze doors, executed, one by Andrea Pisano, and the two others by Ghiberti, which were declared by Michael Angelo to be worthy of being the gates of Paradise. Upon these gates are represented in most beautiful style, the principal events in the life of the Saviour, together with the leading subjects of the Old Testament; while the frame-work is filled with statues and busts of patriarchs, saints, and prophets. The statues of Miriam and Judith are particularly beautiful. The great Dante was a native of Florence, and delighted to visit this sacred edifice. In his "Divina Commedia," he often speaks of it. On one occasion while in the Baptistery, a child had fallen into one of the fonts, which are always kept full of holy water, and in order to save the child he broke the font. In the nineteenth chapter of his Inferno, he alludes to it:

> "Those basins formed for water to baptize;
> One of the same, I broke some years ago,
> To save a drowning child; be this my word
> A seal, the motive of my deed to show."

The cupola is covered with immense mosaics, representing a gigantic figure of our Lord on his judgment-seat dispensing justice; beneath is Lucifer, with his huge, fiery mouth wide open, into which has just been thrust a poor wretch, who could not give a good account of his acts at the "awful bar of God." It is my great delight to visit this group of magnificent buildings every morning. The Cathedral, the Campanile, the Baptistery! such a group is nowhere, on the habitable globe, to be found. All encased with marble, all towering far up into the blue heavens, all having lived for more than four centuries, and will, no doubt, stand upon the quiet banks of the Arno, till " earth shall pass away, and time shall be no more."

There are nearly 200 churches in Florence; the people, of course, being *exceedingly pious.* Among these churches, the most remarkable are San Lorenzo, Santa Croce, the Annunziata, San Marco, and Santa Maria Novella. In San Lorenzo is is buried Cosimo de Medici, the " Pater patriæ " of Florence. His body was deposited in front of the high altar in the pavement, and the spot is marked by a circular space of inlaid green and red porphyry. Adjoining the north transept is an apartment devoted to the monuments of Lorenzo the Magnificent, and his son, by Michael Angelo. They are the most famous works of this great master, and attract more visitors to Florence, perhaps, than any other objects of high monumental art. Lorenzo is represented seated in his tomb, with his head resting on his hand, in a position of deep thought; the two figures reclining at his feet are Aurora and Twilight, or night and morning. The whole group have a very affecting influence on the beholder, and you go away utterly astonished and amazed at the power of the master-artist, in giving such expression to dull, cold marble. Back of the choir is the celebrated Medician chapel. This is a lovely room, completely encrusted with Florentine mosaics. Here, coral and cornelian, jasper, agate, lapis lazuli, and chalcedony, vie with each other, and assume all the artistic shapes and colors that the ingenuity of man can contrive, or the most prurient fancy conceive. The ceiling is beautifully done in fresco, and the floors blaze in the most gorgeous marbles. I doubt whether Aladdin ever dreamed of such a room as this, and am certain that he had no such apartment in the palace which he built for his beautiful bride.

In the church of Santa Croce, lie the mortal remains of the illustrious dead. Here are Dante, and Michael Angelo, and Alfieri, and Machiavelli; four names that have filled the Italian trump of fame for ages. They all lie quietly in this old church, objects of great veneration and regard. Although in the silent tomb, their works still live, and are destined to instruct and please for ages to come.

To-day is Sunday, and I spent the evening at the Casino—the Hyde Park of Florence. It is a lovely spot, and is delightfully situated on the banks of the Arno, just outside the city as you pass through the Porta al Prato. Here all Florence drive out of an evening, and show off their fine equipages. There is a great deal of style here, more than in any other part of Italy. Four-horse coaches, with liveries, outriders, &c., are very common. The man who seemed to *splurge* the most was an American, fresh from California, with his pockets *full of rocks*. I regret that I did not have time to visit Vallambrosa, 18 miles distant, and Fiesole, the quondam residence of our old friend Galileo, the star-gazer, who first entertained that foolish notion that the earth moved instead of the sun, notwithstanding Joshua told the sun " to stand and deliver." I find it, however, impossible to spend any more time here.

The manufactures of Florence have fallen off very much; they still, however, do a good deal in silks and woollens, in straw hats, porcelain, and mosaics. The chief dependence of the city is on the visits and temporary residence of foreigners. The artists, also, form quite a large portion of the population, and add much to the income of the resident citizens.

All Florence to-day is in a great state of excitement. The arms of Piedmont have just been placed on the ducal palace, while large handbills are stuck up on every corner of the street, " Viva Victor Emanuel!" "Death to the house of Lorraine." The Grand Duke has long since fled to his cousin at Vienna. He and his son were at the battle of Solferino. This has given mortal offence to the Tuscans, who would, I believe, cut him to pieces, if he were to return. The Italians will fight now, and no mistake. They are fully aroused at last, and are raising a voluntary subscription to buy one million stand of arms, to place in the hands of the people. Garibaldi is in Bologna. He goes to Modena to-morrow, with a part of his troops. He is the beau-ideal—the Chevalier Bayard—of Italian chivalry, and is rallying the whole country around him. The Tuscans deserve to be free. I hope Napoleon will say to Austria, "Hands off."

To-day, Florence has had a complete revolution, without a mob, without an accident even. She has voluntarily joined the fortunes of Victor Emanuel, and will prove true in any emergency.

I cannot close this letter without expressing my gratitude to Mr. Powers and Mr. Hart, our American sculptors, for their kindness to me. Mr. Hart is a *regular brick*. I hope I may have it in my power to entertain him some day at Allandale. Adieu.

Yours truly,

H. W. A.

LETTER NO. XXIX.

Hotel d'Angleterre, Rome, Italy,
Oct. 13, 1859.

Editors Advocate:

I am in the "Eternal City" at last, and have now arrived at the "ultima thule" of my journey. I arrived here five days since, and have been busily engaged in visiting the various curiosities of this city of the Cæsars. Rome is divided by the river Tiber into two unequal parts. This river is a small, muddy stream, about as wide as the Atchafalaya, at Simms Port, but not so deep. Take out St. Peter's and the Vatican, the Quirinal Palace and the Coliseum, and Rome becomes a miserable concern, a one-horse town. By-the-by, I am travelling through Italy with two very clever English gentlemen; one Mr. Forsyth, an eminent lawyer of London, and the other the Rev. Mr. Robertson, an elegant scholar, and a prebendary of Canterbury. They are social, good companions. We met in Florence, and have concluded to "tie to one another," in this land of *barbarians*, where you never hear the mother tongue of a white man and a Christian spoken! I made the remark to-day that Rome was a one-horse town. These gentlemen immediately pulled out their memorandum-books, and put it down, saying, " Well, that will do for America!" The streets here are filthy and narrow; the houses generally mean and dirty, while the beggars and fleas are as thick as "leaves in Vallambrosa."

The Italians are a far different race of human beings from their Roman ancestors. When imperial Cæsar ruled Rome, it contained 4,000,000 of inhabitants. Now this once great city is not as large as St. Louis, or Cincinnati, or New Orleans; only numbering 150,000 inhabitants, the beggars and priests all told. The present modern city is built on the Campus Martius of the old Romans. With but few exceptions, the houses are badly constructed, and kept in worse repair. There is no Yankee thrift here. Prodigality and poverty go hand in hand, and the most assiduous and importunate beggars follow you into the very church of St. Peter.

Of course the first great object of attraction to all visitors, is the Cathedral. It is not only the great wonder of Rome and all Italy, but stands confessedly far superior to any thing in the shape of a church ever constructed by man. The far-famed temple of Ephesus could not be compared to it. Nor can the temple of Solomon, built of the "fir-tree and the cedar of Lebanon, and covered with gold," be considered equal to this wonderful pile. It exceeds the most extravagant conception of the human mind. It is 607 feet long, 445 feet wide, and 458 high! and the interior is one solid mass of variegated marble. The large pictures for the altars are all of mosaic, copied from the great masters in the Vatican. They are so well executed that I was entirely deceived, and could not be made to believe it, till I had given them a minute inspection. The statuary is all of colossal size, and by those immortal artists, Michael Angelo, Canova, Bernini, Thorwaldsen, Teudon, Algardi, etc., etc. Around the base or lower rim of the cupola, are these words, in huge mosaic letters: "Tu es Petrus et hanc petram ædificabo ecclesiam meam et tibi dabo claves regni cœlorum." Notwithstanding the church is so large, still the proportions are so good and harmonious, and the windows so well arranged, that instead of dark and dreary walls, as at Milan and Florence, all is cheerful and bright, warm and luxurious. If the surroundings have any effect upon the human heart, and fit it for a closer communion with our Heavenly Father, then most assuredly St. Peter's possesses far greater advantages than all other churches I have ever seen. I noticed that there are no tinsel trinkets, or pinchbeck ornaments hung around the necks of the saints and the Madonnas, but all is in good taste; every thing is of gold or silver, Carrara marble or bronze. The façade of the church is built entirely of travertine, (a white limestone.) It is 379 feet long and 148 high. It has three stories and an attic. Each story has nine windows and heavy balconies, from which the pope bestows his benedictions on festival days. On the attic are 13 colossal statues, each 18 feet high, which represent the Saviour and the 12 apostles. The colonnade in front of the church is so well contrived as to conceal the buildings on each side of the piazza. This is considered the masterpiece of the great Bernini. The colonnades are semicircular, 55 feet wide, having 4 rows of columns 48 feet high, and so arranged as to admit two carriages abreast, between the inner rows. The number of columns is 284. On the entablature stand 192 statues, each 12 feet high. The area inclosed by these two colonnades, in its greatest diameter, is 787 feet. The colonnades terminate in two galleries 360 feet long by 23 wide, leading to the vestibule of St. Peter's.

As you enter the church, at the bottom of the steps are placed by the present pope (Pius IX.) two colossal statues. The one on the right is St. Peter, that on the left St. Paul. In the centre of the piazza, in front, is the Egyptian obelisk, and on each side is a beautiful fountain, eternally throwing up its cool, refreshing waters, inviting all to come and drink. The ascent to the top of the dome of St. Peter's, is by a broad, spiral staircase, paved with marble, which leads you up so gently that you could easily go up on horseback. On the walls of this staircase, as you go along, are inserted tablets, commemorating the time when distinguished sovereigns made the ascent. No one can give any idea of the immensity of St. Peter's, unless he visits the top. Here are spread out *acres* of roof and cupolas, without number; but I saw no carpenters' houses, with their families, on the top of St. Peter's. This is a generally received impression, found in guide-books, but it is all in my eye Elizabeth M. It is no such thing. The roof is of Roman cement, and is as clean and free of any incumbrance as the slate covering of any sugar-house in West Baton Rouge. From the main roof, covered with copper taken from the Pantheon, you ascend the dome. It is double, that is, an inner and an outer dome. The stairs are between, admitting only one person at a time. Round and round you go, higher and higher, up—up, until at last you reach the *ball*, on which stands the cross. By a perpendicular iron ladder you pass up into the ball. It is 8 feet in diameter, and will hold 16 persons. It is made of sheets of copper. The cross comes next, and is 16 feet in height. On descending I lingered some time on the main roof, and with glass in hand, enjoyed a view which is alone vouchsafed to those who make pilgrimages to the shrine of St. Peter. On one side lay the Appenines and the Alban Hills, while on the other were the blue waters of the Mediterranean Sea. The wide and desolate Campagna was spread around in every direction, and you fancied you could smell the foul atmosphere from the adjacent Pontine Marshes.

From this lofty standpoint every object of interest in the city can be easily distinguished, and from this favored spot the setting sun is distinctly seen, as he seeks his watery bed in the bosom of the sea.

From St. Peter's I went to the Tiber, the yellow Tiber, and spent an hour on its muddy shores. The Castle of St. Angelo stands on its banks, and is protected by all the appliances of walls and bastions, drawbridges, etc., which make it impregnable. It is at present filled with French troops, and is under the command of Gen. Guyon. The Tiber is not at this present writing "troubled," nor is "she chafing with her shores," as she was when Cæsar and Cassius swam *her*, although it is a rapid and filthy-looking stream, and I should think a very congenial place for loggerhead turtles and mud cats. There is no poetry about this river. It smells too bad.

From this unsavory river I wended my way slowly to my hotel, where I got a most excellent dinner, (they live well in Rome;) after which I lit a cigar, and strolled down the Corso, in search of amusement for the evening. I had not gone far before I met with my friends Forsyth and Robertson, who proposed to go to the Coliseum, and to the Coliseum we went. This is an immense ruin, and stands the proudest monument of Rome's ancient glory. The people who could conceive of, plan, and build such an immense affair, must have been an immense people. We have nothing like it in our country, not even the custom-house in New Orleans, which, when completed, is to be, I am told, one of the wonders of the world. As we approached the grand old ruin by moonlight, and anticipated so much pleasure in threading its corridors and arches, and viewing its interior by torchlight, we were abruptly stopped by the shrill voice of a French sentinel—" Qui va la ?" We replied, "Americans," and received the pleasing answer, "Approchez, Messieurs." We were very politely informed that the commanding general had ordered that no one should enter the Coliseum after night; but that we could walk around it in every direction as long as we pleased. We availed ourselves of this, and spent an hour or two in viewing this "king of ruins," by the light of an Italian moon.

On my way back to the hotel, I discovered at least *forty* separate and distinct stinks or bad smells, which appear to infest Rome, and come out mostly at night. With the aid of a long moustache, and a much longer segar, I managed, however, to get safe to my room, and in a few minutes I found myself in the land of dreams—a-dreaming of Romulus and Remus and the she-wolf—of Livy and Tacitus and Horace—and my old schoolmaster, Philo Calhoun, who used to flog me most unmercifully on account of not *knowing exactly* what these aforesaid old heathen wrote about. I awoke, however, in the morning, refreshed with a sound and pleasant sleep, ready for work.

He who wishes to learn must labor. The lazy traveller had better stay in Paris, and while away his time on the elegant Boulevards, and in the luxurious cafés. And thus was spent my first day in Rome. I shall write you again in a day or two. When I leave here I shall turn my face homewards, and hurry back as fast as steam can carry me.

Adieu. Truly yours,
H. W. A.

LETTER NO. XXX.

Hotel d'Angleterre, Rome, Italy,
Oct. 15, 1859.

Editors Advocate:

Since writing you a day or two ago, I have seen a good deal more of this interesting old city. I find that instead of tiring here, one becomes more interested daily, the more he sees. The Vatican claims the first attention of artists visiting Rome, for here, in its endless galleries, are seen the best specimens of antique art. It is an immense pile of buildings, all joined together in one palace, being 1,151 feet long and 767 feet wide, thus covering about 15 acres of ground! From this must be taken, of course, the small courts, or flower-gardens, in the centre of the palace. There are, in this remarkable palace over 4,000 rooms: what in the d—l they do with them all, is more than I can tell! The pope is not married, and consequently has no wife and children; Antonelli, his prime minister, is also an old bachelor, who is pro-

hibited by his vows from even batting his eye at
the prettiest girl in all Rome. This palace joins
St. Peter's Church, and also has a covered secret
walk to the castle of St. Angelo, so that in case the
Vatican should ever get too hot for his Holiness,
he can *rat it* down to the castle, and get under the
big guns. The statuary and paintings of the Vatican have a world-wide celebrity. The "Apollo
Belvidere," and the "Laocoon," are antique treasures, which all the mines of California could not
purchase. In a room adjoining the Apollo are the
"Athletes," and "Perseus with the Head of Medusa," by Canova, but they cannot be compared
to the Apollo. For ages, thousands of modern artists have attempted to make copies of the original,
but none have ever equalled it. The Apollo stands
pre-eminently the very first in the sculptor's art.
It is the perfect form of a full-grown, fine-looking,
active, healthy man. The face is Grecian, and its
features are highly expressive and very handsome,
and pleasing to look at. In fact, it is just such a
face and such a figure as any sensible woman, with
good taste, would fall in love with. On the contrary, the Laocoon is painful to behold. It is, by
artists, considered as a fine subject for the study of
anatomy. The serpents have entwined themselves
around the father and his two sons in such a close
embrace, that the most intense agony is depicted
in their countenances. It is all cut from one block
of marble. These two statues have elegant apartments appropriated to themselves, separate and

apart from the rest, and are daily honored with crowds of visitors. In the Capitol is one statue that deserves to be classed along with them; it is the "Dying Gladiator." This statue made a greater impression on my mind than all the rest. The cold marble almost seems to speak, and to tell the sympathizing stranger the sadness that oppresses the soul of the dying man, while his wife and children are far away on the banks of the Danube.

The "Infant Hercules," in the Vatican, is a fine piece of antique statuary, in a most admirable state of preservation. The face, the form, the stout *pins* —in fact, the whole figure, is an exact likeness of a distinguished young lawyer, formerly of West Baton Rouge, but now of Iberville. There is also here, a bust of the Emperor Vespasian, which is as much like W. W. Lemmen, Esq., of West Baton Rouge, as if it had been made for him by Michael Angelo, or Antonio Canova. In every species of statuary this gallery is the richest in the world. From a contemplation of every thing that is grand, and even sublime, in the way of sculpture, you pass on into the Egyptian Museum. This is very extensive. Huge lions and enormous sphinxes, marble sarcophagi and granite crocodiles, mummied cats and mummied babies, with a thousand and one other Egyptian curiosities, almost bewilder the visitor, as he plods his weary way through the long and silent corridors. Further on, you see immense antique vases of malachite and granite, together with huge allegorical statues, which astonish you not only with the grandeur, but with the vastness of the ancient Romans.

The way from the statuary to the paintings is short and direct, and when once you have been permitted to set your eyes on the paintings of the Vatican, you may go home and say you are satisfied with oil and canvas, for you have seen it all! There are not as many paintings in this gallery as at Florence, but they are all gems. The pride of the gallery, of course, is the "Transfiguration," by Raphael. It is painted on wood, and is generally considered by artists to be the finest painting in the world. It is, indeed, astonishing to look at. The more you see it, the longer you want to look at it. The painting contains 27 figures. The Saviour is transfigured in the clouds, on either side are Moses and Elias, and below are the apostles and the people. In this great painting are two figures which stand out so prominently, and are so unlike, that you can never forget them. The one is the divine, sweet face of the Saviour, and the other is the pale, bluish, unearthly countenance of the boy that is possessed of a devil, and brought by his father to be healed.

Next comes the great painting of "The Communion of St. Jerome," by Domenichino. St. Jerome died at Bethlehem, and is receiving the sacrament from St. Ephraim of Syria; Santa Paola is on her knees, kissing the hands of the dying saint; the Arab and the lion give variety to the composition, and identify the scene in which the representation is laid. In the same room is the "Madonna da Foligno," one of Raphael's greatest efforts. Room No. 4 contains Titian's best pieces—his "Madonna and Child," his "St. Sebastian," and "St. Francis with the Cross." Here, also, are the most sublime works of Guido, Poussin, Correggio, Caravaggio, Perugino, and Guercino. In passing out of the Vatican you meet the French soldiers with their eternal red breeches; they guard the very doors of St. Peter's—in fact, rule Rome; for Gen. Guyon is just as much master of this city as ever Augustus Cæsar was.

I took a long ride to-day, way out to the Alban Hills, through the desert-like Campagna. I went by the celebrated "Appian Way," and found it to be a very ordinary, narrow road, only 14 feet wide, paved with lava, and not half so good as the shell road in New Orleans. The tombs of the Scipios are near this road. They are built like so many cells under ground, and present a very dark and gloomy appearance. They are dug in the native tufa, without arches of brick or stone, and may be considered as a species of catacombs on a small scale. I stopped at the tomb of old Africanus, (for his ashes are here,) and wished his soul a happy time, in company with the best gods of ancient Rome, for old Africanus was a trump!

There is not much beauty in Rome; occasionally you meet with a pretty face. The women here, by a strange coincidence, all appear to be *enceinte* at this present writing. Why so, I cannot tell.

The desert Campagna, which surrounds Rome on all sides, is filled with ruins—immense ruins—with occasional olive trees. This tree seems to grow here indigenous, and without any cultivation whatever. It attains, in the Campagna, a very large size, and affords shade to the huge white oxen, which are reared here in great numbers. In my last letter I spoke of the Colisuem; since which time I have visited it frequently, and spent much time on its immense walls. It is a huge affair. The area contained in this monster amphitheatre is six acres; the walls are 157 feet high, and of vast thickness. When this enormous structure was in its palmiest days under the reign of Titus, there could be seated in it 80,000 people at one time. Here were gladiatorial sports kept up for the amusement of the people, and here many a primitive Christian was torn to pieces by wild beasts, to grace a Roman holiday. Notwithstanding many modern palaces have been built from the ruins of this "mighty relic," still it is in a good state of preservation, and is now protected by the civil authorities, who keep soldiers stationed there day and night. The Baths of Titus are close by, and are built on the same grand scale. Although nearly two thousand years old, still the frescos on the arches are, in many places, as fresh and beautiful as ever. The modern Romans seem to have but little reverence for the classic works of their ancestors. The once beautiful Temple of Minerva is now a baker's shop, where black bread and villanous macaroni are sold.

The Pantheon is a wonderful building. It has a portico of sixteen granite columns, with white marble Corinthian caps. The centre of the immense dome is still left open at the top. It is used as a church, and here lie the remains of the great Raphael. The portico of the Pantheon is considered to be the most perfect specimen of ancient architecture now in existence. The column of Trajan is one of the " lions " of Rome, and stands unrivalled for beauty of proportion and elegant bas-reliefs. From this, no doubt, Napoleon I. took his design for the column at the Place Vendôme, in Paris. The Corso is the fashionable street along which, every evening, elegant carriages are seen driving to the Piazza del Popolo. Just above this piazza is the Pincian Hill, which is ascended by a winding way. On the top are most elegant gardens, filled with fountains and flowers. Here the *elite* of Rome assemble every evening to listen to the French Imperial band. From this beautiful garden all Rome lies before you as a map, and you can easily count the famous seven hills on which the city is built. Here, also, is the place to see the famous Italian sunset. Believe me, it is all a humbug, for the skies are no brighter here than in Louisiana.

The pope resides during the winter at the Vatican. He left on yesterday, for his summer residence in the country. I had just crossed the Tiber on my way to St. Peter's, when his carriage came along, heralded by his Swiss body guards. I got out of my cab, and took a good look at his Holiness. He put his hand out of the window and blessed the people as he passed along, most of whom fell on their knees. He is regarded here as a good man, but as weak as he is good, in permitting himself to be ruled by his prime minister, Antonelli. The Perugia affair was a very bad piece of business, and has injured his Holiness very much in the estimation of his own people. You will remember that, a few months since, the people of Perugia, like the people of Bologna, and other Papal States, expelled the Pope's legates, and threw off the Papal government. It was during the war between the French and Austrians, when all Italy was unsettled. The Pope sent 2,000 Swiss soldiers to punish the people of Perugia, and whip them into allegiance again. They fell upon the unarmed village, and killed, wounded, and robbed indiscriminately. Many women and children were brutally murdered, and much property destroyed. Instead of censuring the brutal soldiery for their horrid murders, he has promoted the commanding officer of the expedition, and distributed medals among the subalterns. I have heard no man in Rome speak an unkind word of the Pope. He is regarded by all classes as a good, conscientious man, exceedingly pious, and amiable, and kind-hearted. But all blame, and even denounce his premier, Antonelli, in most violent language, as the author of all the evils of the present government. Affairs here, at present, are very complicated. If it were not for French bayonets, the Pope could not stay in Rome twenty-four hours. The people—the masses—the rich and poor, the high and low, are all opposed to the present Papal government, and are crying aloud for reform, but Antonelli will not give an inch. He is proud and haughty, cruel and vindictive.

> "The day will come—that great avenging day,
> When Troy's proud glory in the dust shall lay;
> When Priam's power and Priam's self shall fall,
> And one prodigious ruin swallow all."

I believe it. Yes, the day will come when the temporal power of the Pope will fall. It ought to fall. Any government that has to be backed up by foreign bayonets; that steadfastly refuses a trial by jury; that seizes state prisoners without a hearing, locks them up in the felon's cell, there to rot, deserves to be rooted out from the face of the civilized earth. I undertake to say, that in Rome and Naples there is less real piety, and more highhanded, unblushing wickedness, than in any other two cities in Christendom.

Rome has 30,000 priests and 10,000 artists! The college of the "Propaganda Fidei" is also crowded. Here are students from all parts of the earth—Malays and Nubians, Hindoos and Japanese, Algerines and Arabs, North American Yankees and South American natives, all mixed up, in long black gowns and three-cornered caps.

I have, since I arrived here, called on our countrywoman, Miss Hosmer. She has already taken a high position as a sculptress, and has just finished in plaster her Zenobia. It is the first ever attempted by any sculptor, I believe, and is a wonderful production for a young woman, and she from New England! Mr. Gibson, the English sculptor, was very kind to me, and was good enough to take me into his studio, and show me his painted or stained Venus, that is creating so much sensation in Rome. It is a very beautiful piece of statuary, and is decidedly new; it being the only one, I believe, ever treated in this manner. It is stained a deep pink color, and attracts much attention and great criticism among the *dilettanti*.

I would like to write you more about Rome, but must close this already long letter. There are so many curiosities here—so many pure fountains, gushing up with cool, refreshing waters—so many many splendid churches—so many grand old ruins —so many pretty contadinas in their bright-colored garments—that Rome becomes a world within itself, and furnishes endless objects of attraction to the classic scholar, the matter-of-fact traveller, or the seeker of fun, frolic, and pleasure. In the Palazzo Borghese, in the Barberini, the Quirinal, and the Colonna, are paintings without number, three of which, alone, would attract more attention than every painting in our country put together; they are "the Beatrice Cenci," by Guido, "the Chase of Diana," by Domenichino, and "the Sacred and Profane Love," by Titian.

This being my last evening in Rome, I paid my respects to, and took *leave* of, the "Apollo" and the "Transfiguration." As I came down the large steps of the Vatican I crossed the Piazza, and took off my hat to St. Peter's; passing the fountain near the Obelisk, I drank freely of its pure and refreshing water, and with hurried step hastened on to the Piazza del Popolo. Here I passed the gate, and in a few moments was seated under the tall pine trees of the Villa Borghese. While the breeze was gently roaring through the pines, I fell asleep and dreamed of home. I saw the black smoke rising from the tall chimneys on the banks of the Mississippi, and heard the loud puff of the sugarmills, mingled with the happy songs of the negroes.

Farewell, Eternal City! Farewell, a long farewell, to thy grandeur and thy glory, to thy stately palaces and grand old ruins! Farewell to thy works of art, on brilliant canvas and pure pale marble! I am tired of you all. I go back to "the land of the west, the beautiful west," where the unsubstantial arts and sciences are but little cultivated, but where land—terra firma—mother earth —is cultivated; where every arpent produces two hogsheads of sugar, and every acre a bale of cotton. Where the plough, the loom, and the anvil are more thought of than the "Apollo Belvidere," the

"Transfiguration," or the "Dying Gladiator;" where the painter is a practical mechanic, and uses his brush, as a painter should, on weather-boards and wagon-wheels, and where the knights of the chisel much prefer white pine and cypress to Carrara marble. Yes, I am returning to the only land of liberty and equality on which the sun shines, and where John Smith and William Muggins are just as much respected as my Lord Tomnoddy, or his Grace the Duke of Tobaccojuice, provided always they are law-abiding citizens, and deport themselves as gentlemen.

Good-bye: I leave to-morrow morning at 6 o'clock, by the train, for Civita Vecchia, and hope to be in Paris in three days and a half.

Truly yours,
H. W. A.

LETTER NO. XXXI.

HOME AGAIN

WEST BATON ROUGE, LA., *Dec.*, 1860.

EDITORS ADVOCATE:

"My home—my home—my happy home—
Spot ever, ever dear to me:
Where'er I go, where'er I roam,
My heart still fondly clings to thee."

After a very long voyage across the "stormy sea," I am at last quietly and comfortably seated at my own hearth-stone, "taking mine case in mine own inn." I hear the loud puff of the sugar-mill, and the cheerful song of the happy negroes at work in the cane-fields. All now is bustle and life on the sugar-coast, for the canes must now be saved or be forever lost. How different are my feelings now, from what they were one short month ago, in the city of London. I hope, my dear sirs, that neither you nor any of your kind readers may ever be sick from home. The Arabs have a parting wish, a kind of benediction, which no one can properly appreciate, unless he has once been on a bed of sickness in the "stranger's land." It is this: "May you die at home among your friends." Now this matter of dying is not a very agreeable subject at any time to think about, and especially when seated upon that "pale horse," the aspect of death is any thing but inviting to a sensible man. . But few that I know of have their "houses set in order," and none are ready to "cross that melancholy flood that poets write of." All dread the road which leads to that "undiscovered country" from whose bourne no traveller has ever yet returned. In a strange land, far away from home, from kindred, and from friends, the heart yearns for even one familiar kind face. If ever friendship's hand is wanted, it is then. If ever affection's smile is needed, then, oh! then is the time.

To Mr. Wm. Forsyth, of Temple Bar, Q. C., a distinguished lawyer of London, I am under lasting obligations. He was kind and attentive to me during my long and severe illness. Mr. Beverly Tucker, our worthy consul at Liverpool, I can never forget; for hearing of my illness, he wrote to friends in London to call and see me, and do every thing requisite for my cure and comfort. These friends paid me every attention, and offered every assistance, and in due course of time I recovered.

From Liverpool I shipped to Boston on board the Cunard steamer Canada, in the very midst of a storm. So great was the anticipated danger, that four passengers who came down to the ship, refused to come on board, giving up their passage-money and their state-rooms, and bidding the captain good-bye, with the consoling remark (to us) that they "didn't care about getting drowned that trip." In going out of the Mersey it blew a perfect hurricane. All dreaded the terrible fate of the East Indiaman, which had gone on the rocks here only a few weeks before, drowning 500 passengers. Our good ship, however, weathered the storm full well, and in the course of 48 hours' hard steaming, we landed in the " Cove of Cork." Here we took in the royal mails, and set out again for the broad Atlantic. We had scarcely struck old Ocean, when the gale began afresh, and then for "twelve long stormy days and stormy nights, we were tossed upon the raging sea." The steamer shipped, as they call it, a great deal of water, generally carrying from eight to ten inches on deck. Of course we were all very sea-sick, and many suffered much. We had on board a Catholic priest from Boston. He was very much frightened during the whole trip, and as each big wave would strike the ship and jar the bulwarks, he would jump up out of his berth and cross himself. On a certain occasion he had gone up into the cabin, and before he could reach a chair, the ship gave a lurch, and threw him head foremost *under the table*. He rose as pale as death, crossed himself, and took his seat. The captain about that time came along, and he said to him, " Captain, how much longer do you think this storm will last?" The captain replied he could not tell, but hoped it would be over in a few days!

"My Lord!" said he, "Captain, you don't think it will last several days longer, do you?" and then he crossed himself again.

"Yes," said the captain, "I think it will last at least a week!"

"Then," cried our poor priest, "there is no hope for me. I have an aged mother in Boston, 87 years old. If this storm does not cease very soon, *she will live longer than I will!*"

But "behind a frowning Providence" there was a smiling face. The good ship arrived safe, and our pious priest, I hope, may live full many a year, to tell his flock of the perils of the sea, and of the saving arm of Him who walks upon the waters of the deep.

I often, in my own mind, draw a comparison between our own country and the old world. True, we have no paintings here, for in the Pitti Palace at Florence, there are more good paintings than on the whole of the American continent. In statuary, also, we are far behind. In the manufactory of silks and satins, fine cloths, poplins, linens and laces, we cannot pretend to compete with the looms of Europe. But in all the articles of actual necessity, such as linseys and jeans, heavy cotton goods and calicoes, farming utensils, boots, shoes, and heavy cutlery, in steam-engines, saw-mills, and all sorts of useful machinery, we are, I am proud to say, a long way ahead of any thing "across the water."

Books are fully as well published with us, and just as well bound, as they are in London, and at least one-half cheaper. For instance, for a copy of the "Idyls of the King," by Tennyson, I paid in Liverpool $2.50. In New York the same book can be had for $1. Taking New York as a fair sample of an American city, and London as a European, I find that four houses are generally better built, and in a much more tasteful and elegant style. There is no such street in London as Fifth Avenue, nor any at all comparable to Broadway. Regent and Oxford Streets are the finest in that great city, but they have no buildings on either of them like the great hotels, or those splendid marble palaces on Broadway. In hotels, we beat the world.

An Englishman is not generally a social being. He prefers his club to a public hotel, and therefore you seldom see him in his native country about a hotel. He orders his mutton-chops, or his roast-beef and potatoes, and quietly by himself eats and drinks to his fill. With an American it is quite different. He puts up at a first-class hotel, for he wants to see his friends. He wants to talk with them, and drink with them, and perhaps to take a "little frolic" with them.

In the large dining-rooms of the St. Nicholas, the Metropolitan, and the Fifth Avenue, you will every day, at about 4 o'clock, P. M., see the most cheerful, the most elegant and agreeable assemblages that the wide world can produce. There are no such hotels in London. There is but one such in Paris, the Hotel du Louvre. It is, however, not properly managed. Their *table d'hôte* is at 6 P. M., and not one-third of the visitors attend it. They generally dine at the restaurants, and breakfast at the *cafés*. I never saw at the dinner-table of the Louvre more than 75 persons. With us 500 guests sit down together in the same dining-saloon. The waiters are so well arranged, that all are duly attended to in proper time. This crowd would run an untravelled Englishman perfectly crazy. He would order more 'alf and 'alf, port-wine, and Scotch whiskey, until he drank himself perfectly oblivious.

It is, however, as an agricultural people, that we excel the rest of the world. The broad acres of corn, and wheat, and oats, and rye; the large fields of tobacco and of rice, the extensive plantations of cotton and sugar-cane, these make the United States the greatest producing community on the face of the earth. We now clothe the world. We could, if it were necessary, not only feed the world, but add to its *sweet* contentment, hogsheads of pure sugar, and " oceans " of molasses.

I met a very intelligent Englishman and his wife in Venice. We were together several days. Said he to me one day, " Sir, I am from Lincolnshire, the great grain-growing county of England. We have there some farmers who cultivate as much as 200 acres of land!" I smiled at this innocent boast, and informed my English friend that in Louisiana there were many planters who cultivated 1,000 acres in cotton, and fully as much in corn and sugar-cane. The well-fed Britisher gave me an incredulous blink of his eye, as if he wished me plainly to understand that there was such a thing in the world as *gassing ;* but when I reminded him that we made 4,000,000 bales of cotton, and 400,000 hogsheads of sugar, he finally agreed that his " American cousins" were a great people.

England imports most of her breadstuffs. Her lands are mostly appropriated to the growth of food for horses and cattle, and to gardening purposes. Indian corn does not do well in any portion of Great Britain. Wheat, rye, barley and potatoes, horse-beans, turnips and beets, and most of all the grasses, are the principal crops. Labor here is cheap, in country and in city. The very best of female labor can be had for 6 shillings per week, or 20 cents per day! No laboring man in Great Britain receives over 40 cents per day, and a great many from 15 to 20 cents; consequently, if you should happen to get out of " l'argent" in the old country, and have not in your possession good letters of credit, whatever sickly sentimentalists and moon-struck philosophers may say to the contrary, you will find that your money is your best friend in a strange land, or in fact any other land.

In England the farmers use a great deal of guano and compost, and other manures. The land is forced to its utmost capacity, for it rents frequently for £5, that is, $25 per acre. These lands are of course valued very high. Most of them can't be bought at any price. The most inferior bring readily $500 per acre.

I saw no Indian corn growing in any part of Europe, except near Vienna and in Italy. On the Mincio and the Po it flourishes well, and that, together with rice, now forms the principal food for the poorer classes in Lombardy.

Our young orators, in their Fourth-of-July speeches, are given to "sail the American eagle" too much. They boast that we could whip the world in arms. Now if these aforesaid "spread-eagle gentry" would only take a short trip to Europe, and see the military strength of only the "four great powers," they would come home perfectly satisfied that we had better attend to our own affairs, and let others alone. I confess, that so far as I am concerned, it took out of me all that extra patriotic conceit which seems to be part and parcel of every American citizen; for beyond the "dark rolling Danube," are millions of people who have never heard of the United States of America! It is true, the name of Washington has gone into every civilized, and even semi-barbarous land, but I met with well-dressed people in Austria, who had never heard of Washington, and when I told them that I was from America, they asked me what America! This certainly bespeaks great ignorance in the Austrian empire, but such is the fact.

We are no doubt a great people, numbering, now, 33,000,000 of inhabitants, a greater population than England, Ireland, and Scotland combined. Our flag is respected on every sea, and our people kindly treated in every land. Americans are popular everywhere. As travellers, they do not interfere with the local governments of the country, but spend their money freely and pass on. While in Leghorn, Florence, or Rome, I felt just as safe as if I had been in my own parlor at home, for the Wabash was in the Mediterranean. She is the finest steamship that ever passed the Straits of Gibraltar, and has given the old fogies of the Levant some idea of the naval power of our country. I know that it has become fashionable, in certain quarters, to say that our government does not give ample protection to her citizens while abroad. Such is not the fact. No government in the world guards and protects the rights of its citizens abroad more than ours at Washington, and I undertake to say, that in Europe no persons are treated as well as Americans.

In music, that is, instrumental, we cannot compare with Dresden and Vienna. In opera, of course Italy and France bear the palm, but in men and women, in the manly form, and the lovely features of the "face divine," we can beat the world.

In London the great masses of the young men are "apprentices." I attended one of their picnics, or holidays, at Hampton Court, and saw about 10,000 assembled together. I have never seen such a large number of such small men assembled together. Not one among the whole number seemed to be 6 feet high, but all below the medium height, delicate and thin. The noble race of Britons is certainly degenerating in the city. In the country they are still robust, strong, and healthy. It is the same way with the women among the working classes. Their haggard and melancholy faces remind me of Tom Hood's "Song of the Shirt." Stitch—stitch—stitch,—work—work—work, is written on every lineament of their pale and care-worn features. Thank God, our black slaves are well fed; they are properly cared for in sickness and in health, and when old age comes on, they are not sent to the poor-house to "linger and to die," but in good warm cabins, in the midst of abundance, and under their master's eye, they live to great old age. I do think that an old negro slave, who has labored faithfully for his master, is the happiest human being of the laboring classes I ever saw. At the age of sixty he is generally free, no labor being required of him. All on the plantation respect and esteem him very highly. His children and grandchildren take pleasure in serving him, while his master and mistress delight in giving him those delicate attentions so grateful to old age. If his mind turns upon religion, he makes the most pious and exemplary Christian, and prays that all on the "old plantation" may at last meet in heaven. From New Orleans to Richmond —from Charleston to St. Louis—you will not find one *black beggar*. How different in London, in Liverpool, in Dublin. In all these great cities they besiege the traveller, and in the most importunate manner appeal to him for bread. Go to the work-house, and there you will see the aged poor crowded together in miserable cells, compelled to work in order to get bread to eat. In every civilized community, the work-house is considered a "house of disgrace." In London it is not, but thousands crowd to it in cold weather, and beg to be admitted; beg for a roof to shelter their white hairs, for fire to warm their aged limbs, for bread to "keep dear life afloat." I have witnessed this misery, this wretchedness, in the streets of the British capital and in her provincial towns, and on returning to my own State I am truly thankful to an overruling Providence, that we have no parsimonious poor-houses, where ragged, starving poverty is farmed out to the lowest bidder; no work-houses, plethoric with aged vice and youthful crime; but that all who wish it, can find employment—all get enough to eat, and that every human being within the broad limits of the State of Louisiana should be contented and happy.

In returning to my own home, I do so perfectly contented, perfectly satisfied. I would not exchange my own humble plantation on the banks of the Mississippi for the proudest barony of old England. As a planter, I much prefer the cultivation of cotton, and corn, and sugar cane, to beets and hops, to turnips and potatoes. As an investment, I am thoroughly satisfied that an acre of sugar cane will produce twice as much—that is, will net double as much—as an acre of any English crop. Still, as an American, I must say that the English are a great people. They possess many noble traits of character, and under a cold and haughty exterior, they carry a warm and generous heart. They have their foolish prejudices, their whims and caprices, but when once you know an Englishman well, break the outer shell, and get into his confidence, you will find him "as sweet as summer and as true as steel."

This letter closes this volume. If the kind reader has been instructed, or even amused, in its perusal, the author's labors will not be entirely lost. At the urgent solicitation of numerous warm friends, he has consented to give his travels to the public. The question is often asked, "How much does it cost to take a trip to Europe?" Now, for the benefit of those who may, at some future day, wish to take the trip, I will give the result of my experience and observation. The table on p. 246 is made out for one who wished to travel in a plain, unpretending style; to stop at the best hotels; enjoy all, and see all, that the most curious or fastidious could desire. From this, you will plainly perceive that a trip to Europe will not cost any more than the usual northern tour, or a season at the Virginia springs. Those who can make up their minds to stand a little sea-sickness, will be most amply repaid, for a warmhearted welcome will await them wherever they go. England claims kin with America, and is daily drawing more closely the bonds of friendship. She looks to us as her natural ally. France has ever been our good friend, and the emperor looks upon Louisiana with especial favor, having many warm personal friends in our midst. In Germany, the students are more than kind to all Americans, and share with you their beer and their pipes. In Italy, an American is perfectly at home, for now the spirit of liberty is abroad in that beautiful land, and an Italian delights to shake by the hand any one who hails from "the land of the free and the home of the brave."

Adieu, Messrs. Editors Advocate. Accept my thanks for your many kindnesses, and ever believe me, Very truly,
Your friend,
H. W. A.

APPENDIX.

ANECDOTES OF TRAVEL.

STRASBOURG, FRANCE.

From Basle I went to Strasbourg, pretty much to see the great clock that works so accurately by its complicated machinery: at 12 o'clock the Apostles walk out in front of the Saviour, and when Peter passes along, the cock (as large as life) crows three times. It is a wonderful piece of mechanism, and hundreds visit the cathedral every day to see it. While seated in the Hotel de Ville, busily engaged in writing a letter to a friend, and smoking a cigar, I would occasionally spit out of the window, which was up, the weather being very warm. There were no spittoons in the room, and I did not wish to spit on the well-carpeted floor—consequently, out of the window into the street I had to spit. Well, in an unguarded moment, as misfortune would have it, I spit smack into the face of a tall, fine-looking Frenchman, who happened just at the moment to turn and look into the window. The Gaul gazed at me at first with an uncertain and vacant stare:

then came a volley of oaths and a violent shaking of fists. I said to him in my very best French, "Pardonnez moi, monsieur—un accident, un accident—un fâcheux accident." This, however, did not satisfy my enraged Frenchman. He swore terribly, not exactly in Dutch, but in Strasbourg French. He launched at my devoted head volley after volley of horrid, guttural oaths, at the close of each, with threatening, clenched fist, he demanded "*satisfaction* —satisfaction." This was on the public street. He was in front and on the outside of the hotel, and I on the inside, talking to him through the window. In the midst of all this, a large assemblage was collected around us. I asked if there was any person present who could speak English. One man said, Yes. I then requested him to say to my Frenchman, that I had spit on him accidentally; that I regretted it very much; that I was an American, having just arrived in Strasbourg, an entire stranger to him and everybody else in the city, and that I hoped my explanation would be satisfactory. This being interpreted to my foaming Frenchman, instead of appeasing his rage, seemed to increase it. Having nursed his wrath during my explanation, it now broke loose afresh, and he demanded with terrific shrieks, " satisfaction—*satisfaction.*" I concluded that the time had come when further forbearance would cease to be a virtue ; so I requested the interpreter, in a loud and determined voice, to say to my now furious Frenchman, " that I had apologized to him for the merest accident, a half a dozen times; that as he would accept of no apology whatever, but was 'freezing for a fight,' that I would accommodate him : to send me his card— that I had rather shoot the top of *his* head off than any other man's I had ever seen." This was interpreted just as I delivered it, but before any thing in the shape of " preliminaries" could be arranged, a policeman stepped up, and touching my adversary on the shoulder, said, very politely, "Voulez-vous aller faire un tour de promenade, monsieur?" Much to my relief, my bloody-minded Frenchman took this "little walk" with the man of authority, but to my utter astonishment, on turning from the window, I found two "buttoned gentlemen," with long swords on, in my room. My landlord was with them, however. I told them, as we sometimes say in Louisiana, that they had better send two to hold the Frenchman— one could hold me, for I wasn't *spoiling* for a fight; that I had rather *drink* any time than shed blood. In a few moments the whole matter was explained and hushed up. I engaged a *valet de place*, and started out sight-seeing, visiting the great cathedral, the tomb of Marshal Saxe, (a noble and splendid work of art,) and the various *factories* where the Strasbourg pies—the patés—are made. All the while, however, I kept a good look-out for my fighting Frenchman. Being of a kind, and, I hope, an amiable disposition, I did not want to kill the man or anybody else; then again, I didn't want him *to kill me*. The idea of being killed in a foreign country, where the English language is not spoken, and where the rights of burial are rather precarious, is somewhat revolting to a sensitive mind. However, the matter all blew over. I spent a very pleasant day in the great city of "sausages and lager bier," and, I must add, of "fighting Frenchmen;" and in the evening took the huge omnibus, and passed through that long avenue of shady trees which leads from Strasbourg to Kehl; thence to Baden Baden, only a few miles, where I found my travelling companion, Dr. Smith, in the midst of a long and heated disputation with a Scotchman. Speaking of spitting on people, &c., it is my duty, as a faithful chronicler of the acts and doings in this European tour, to state that my friend Ed. Johnson got out of a similar case much better than I did. He and Mrs. Johnson, Shelby and myself, were in a car to ourselves, going from Edinboro' to London. We had paid the conductor not to let any other passengers enter our car, as the weather was very hot; and we were getting along very finely, when on a sudden the conductor presented himself at the window, out of which, at the same time, Johnson happened to spit. The man, of course, was spit upon. He said, in *rather* a dissatisfied manner, "You see you have spit upon me." Johnson ran his hand in his pocket, " he put in his thumb," and instead of " pulling out a plum," he pulled out a few shillings, and said to the conductor, " How much is it?" The man said, " Any thing you please, sir." Johnson handed him a couple of shillings, and our conductor thanked and smiled, and bowed himself away. All of which, I think, was very handsomely done.

LONDON.

Before quitting London, I concluded that I would rise very early one morning, and drive down to see the Fish Market, and that celebrated place called " Billingsgate." I issued forth from my hotel (the Trafalgar) before sunrise, and called the first cab or " Hansom," as they are called—a concern that goes on two wheels, with the driver behind outside, and the reins passing over your head. Well, into this Hansom I got, and started off for Billingsgate. After driving several miles, my Jehu pulled up, and gave me the pleasing information that we were at the Fish Market or Billingsgate, which is all the same. I got out and went the rounds; saw the splendid salmon and the delicious sole, the blue fish and the rock; saw boatloads of lobsters, and oysters, and other shell-fish. Having spent an hour walking through the market, I went back to my Hansom, and I found that the carts of the fishmongers had completly surrounded my driver, and there he stood at bay; the fishmongers and their wives heaping curses on his head, as a villanous prig, who had dared to bring his painted "go-cart" into the classic grounds of Billingsgate. The police interfered, and after some time spent in cursing, swearing, and d——ing one another's eyes generally, (all right, for we are in Billingsgate,) he succeeded in extricating my driver, who, "with 'bated breath and whispering humbleness," begged me for God's sake never again to take him among "those heathen devils." I told him to drive on to "the Old Bailey." Arriving there, I spent a few moments in examining that ancient establishment, once redolent with crime and sharp practising lawyers, but now converted into a prison-house for those convicted of capital offences. On leaving "the Old Bailey," we drove on towards the hotel. In passing up the Strand, I saw a gentleman walking very rapidly down the street, and immediately recognized him, I thought, as an English sugar-buyer or broker, who was in the habit of visiting West Baton Rouge, and buying sugars for the English market. I passed my arm over the reins and stopped the horse, telling my driver at the same time to hold on a while, till I could speak to a friend. Getting out of my Hansom, I hurried on in pursuit of my supposed acquaintance. I overtook him, and found him to be walking in a very gingerly manner, as if he had a little touch of the gout or stringhalt, and after looking at his profile some time, I was sure that I had my man; so without further ceremony I gave him a hard slap on the shoulder, and cried out, "Old fellow, how are you?" The gentleman turned upon me with an astonished look, and gave me a freezing stare. Before he could say a word, I remarked that I supposed he had forgotten me; that my name was Capt. A. of West Baton Rouge, and that I had entertained him often at my house. The gentleman opened his eyes the wider, and said that he had no recollection of ever seeing me before. Now, the name of the sugar-buyer was Prescott. I could not at the time recollect his name, so I said to the gentleman, "You say you never saw me before. Were you never in West Baton Rouge? Don't you know Dan Hickey, and haven't we all had many a frolic together at the Brusli Landing?" "No, sir," said he, very quietly, "I never was in West Baton Rouge or the Brusli Landing, and don't know Mr. Dan Hickey!" Thinking that this gentleman might possibly be a brother of the sugar-buyer, I asked him his name. Said he, "Sir, my name is Palmerston." "What! Lord Palmerston?" "Yes, the same." I raised my hat to his lordship, and apologized for annoying him. I told him I was a stranger, an American, travelling for information and for pleasure, and had mistaken him for the person alluded to above. The premier smiled at my mistake, and gave me to understand that he was always glad to make the acquaintance of Americans. He asked me if I had yet visited the Houses of Parliament. I told him I had. He then insisted that whenever I visited them again, if I would only send him my card, he would issue a special permit for my admittance to hear the debates in the House of Commons, for all of which I thanked him, and we, that is, Lord Palmerston and myself, parted, *I hope, good friends.*

MAGENTA, ITALY.

A young gentleman, not by the name of "Guppy," but of Hall, a very intelligent lawyer of California, left Milan with me. We stopped at Magenta, only ten or twelve miles distant, where we spent the day looking at that dread battle-field, so recently drenched with human gore. As we got out of the cars and were going into the depot, we were attacked by a large yellow dog. Both of us drew our sword-canes and determined to give the "canine individual" a good dose of well-tempered steel. A gentleman, however, called the dog off, and as we approached, he said that the dog would not bite us: it was only a way he had of barking at all strangers. Said he, "That dog has a strange history." In the mean time the dog came forward, and seemed by his actions anxious to learn who we were. But to his history: he was the favorite and constant companion of Gen. Espinasse of the Zouaves, who was killed at this place in the recent great battle fought here. When he fell, his dog, true to his nature, stayed by his side. After the battle was over, the General was taken to a room in the depot. Here he died, and when he was buried, the faithful dog followed his master to his grave, and there howled his mournful dirge. The dog went from the grave back to the room in which his master died, and has refused ever since to sleep anywhere else. Even now, as often as the cars stop, and passengers get out, he comes up and smells them, and with eager looks still hopes to find his devoted master. The brave dog bears evidence of the battle, for I noticed in one of his legs a musket-ball not yet extracted. While in Magenta we had quite a time. In order to get to the hotel we had to go through a butcher's shop, and then a livery stable; but when once in the upper story, we found a pleasant place, and had a most delightful breakfast of figs, melons, and grapes, with good country wine. Since the battle here, hundreds come to see the "foughten field," and carry away some relic, generally in the shape of Minié rifle-balls, or brass ornaments from Austrian hats. Already even these have been exhausted, and now, as is the case at Waterloo, they are manufactured for the occasion, buried in the earth until they become rusty, and offered by importunate venders as bona-fide relics gathered from the very identical spot where McMahon charged the Austrians.

H. W. A.

COST OF A TRIP TO EUROPE.

Below will be found an accurate and detailed statement of the cost of a trip to Europe. I speak "from the card," for each and every one of these items was paid by me.

From New Orleans to New York,	$60 00
" New York to Liverpool,	125 00
" Liverpool to London,	6 00
" London to Dover	3 00
" Dover to Calais,	2 00
" Calais to Paris,	4 00
" Paris to Lyons,	7 50
Amount carried forward,	$207 50

APPENDIX. 217

	Amount brought forward	$207	50
From	Lyons to Geneva, Switzerland,	2	50
"	Geneva to Chamouni, Savoy, (diligence,)	2	00
"	Chamouni to Martigny, (by mule,) and across the Alps,	4	00
"	Martigny to Bouveret at Lake Geneva,		50
"	Bouveret to Lake Neuchatel,	1	50
"	Lake Neuchatel to Interlaken and Brientz,	1	50
"	Brientz to Lucerne, (by mule,)	2	00
"	Lucerne by rail to Berne, capital of Switzerland,	2	00
"	Berne to Zurich,	2	50
"	Zurich to Basle,	1	50
"	Basle to Heidelberg,	3	00
"	Heidelberg to Baden Baden,	1	00
"	From Baden Baden to Frankfort-on-the-Main,	2	00
"	Frankfort to Wiesbaden,	1	00
"	Wiesbaden to Mayence,		50
"	Mayence down the Rhine by boat—passing the vineyards of Johannisberger, and Marcobruner, and Hockheimer—passing Coblentz and Bon to Cologne, (Prussia,)	2	50
"	Cologne to Aix-la-Chapelle, through tunnel 6,000 feet in length,	1	50
"	Aix to Brussels,	2	25
"	Brussels to Antwerp, Belgium,		50
"	Antwerp to Rotterdam,	1	50
"	Rotterdam to Amsterdam, by way of the Hague and Leyden,	1	60
"	Amsterdam to Utrecht,	1	50
"	Utrecht to Berlin, Prussia,	11	10
"	Berlin to Leipsic,	1	75
"	Leipsic to Dresden,	2	00
"	Dresden to Prague,	2	40
"	Prague to Vienna,	6	96
"	Vienna to Trieste,	9	50
"	Trieste to Venice, by steamer,	2	50
"	Venice, by Padua, Verona, and Solferino, to Milan,	3	65
"	Milan, by Magenta and Turin, and Alessandria to Genoa,	5	50
"	Genoa to Leghorn, by steamer,	3	00
	Amount carried forward,	$284	71

Amount brought forward, . . . $284 71
From Leghorn to Florence, by Pisa, ... 1 00
" Florence to Civita Vecchia, back by rail, and then steamer, ... 2 50
" Civita Vecchia to "Imperial Rome," . . . 75
$298 96

Thus it will be seen that the actual cost of travel from New Orleans to Rome is precisely $298 96. No more, no less, and at the same time passing through nearly the whole of Europe. The cost of returning to Paris by the Mediterranean to Marseilles, is much cheaper.

From Rome to Marseilles, by steamer, ... $25 00
" Marseilles to Paris, 72 francs, ... 17 25
" Paris to Liverpool, by London, ... 14 50
Passage from Liverpool to New York, . . . 125 00
" " New York to New Orleans, home again, . 60 00
$540 71

For a trip of three months—say 90 days—we will allow the traveller to spend $5 per day. This will cover all his expenses, wines and operas included, unless he should see proper to join the eager throng in the "Conversation Rooms" at Baden Baden, and try his luck at "Rouge et Noir." In that event, there is no telling "what is on the cards." For 90 days at $5 per day, ... 450 00
$990 71

A prudent traveller will not risk his money at cards in a strange land. It is bad enough at home. That being the case, no man needs more than $1,000 to take the extensive trip marked out above. This takes you through the very heart of Europe, and in most of the extravagant capitals. In France and Germany and Austria the fare is good and cheap. In Italy you can live for almost nothing. In Florence I took my breakfast at the best café in the city, and it never exceeded 20 cents! In a tour of three months you cannot spend any more money legitimately than the figures set down. Of course you can throw away just as much as you please. In passing through Geneva, you can step into a jeweller's and order diamond rings and brooches, and enamelled jewelled watches of the latest style; you can fill your pockets in Florence and Rome with cameos and mosaics, and when you get back to Paris you can go on the Boulevards des Italiens, to the "emperor's tailors," and they will fill your trunk with magnificent clothes. You may give dinners at the "Trois Frères Provenceaux," and drive your "liveried establishment" in Hyde Park; but when you return home, you will find that it will take "the big end" of a good-sized sugar crop to foot the bills. In taking this trip, no one will need more than one thousand dollars, unless he wishes to *splurge*: then my advice is, take all you can carry, for you will want every dollar in due course of time.

H. W. A.

www.ingramcontent.com/pod-product-compliance
Lightning Source LLC
Chambersburg PA
CBHW021355230426

43666CB00006B/536